Cracking
College
Admissions

2nd Edition

Cracking
College
Admissions

2nd Edition

Edited by

John Katzman and

The Staff of The Princeton Review

Random House, Inc.

New York

www.PrincetonReview.com

Princeton Review Publishing, L. L. C.
2315 Broadway
New York, NY 10024
E-mail: bookeditor@review.com

ISBN 0-375-76415-1

Editorial Director: Robert Franek
Editor: David Daniel
Designer: Scott Harris
Production Editor: Vivian Gomez
Production Coordinator: Greta Blau

Manufactured in the United States of America.
9 8 7 6 5 4 3 2 1
Second Edition

TABLE OF CONTENTS

EXTENDED TABLE OF CONTENTS

Chapter Three: Grades and Activities 87

Chapter Four: Your Applications 113

Chapter Five: Essays, Recommendations, and Interviews 133

Chapter Six: Minorities, Athletes, Artists, and Other Special Cases 167

INTRODUCTION

When college admissions officers, high school guidance counselors, and how-to-get-into-college books describe the perfect college applicant, they all describe more or less the same person. The ideal candidate, they say, has good grades, high scores, solid extracurricular activities (editor of the newspaper *and* captain of the football team), a fascinating after-school job (teaching English to immigrant children), terrific hobbies (managing a food relief program in Africa *and* playing medieval instruments), and a shelf filled with awards for everything from writing poetry to playing tennis. This candidate also lives on a farm, conducts unusual physics experiments, holds an elected political office in his town, restores old houses, coaches a Little League baseball team, and never once mentions SAT scores during an interview.

Real college applicants sometimes become depressed when they compare this larger-than-life applicant with their own meager selves. But their depression seldom lasts beyond the first day of their freshman year in college, when they notice that their roommates are just as ordinary as they are and that virtually everyone else in their dormitory is ordinary too.

Although it is perfectly true that the ideal candidate would be accepted in a second by any college in the United States, it is also true that ideal candidates are in short supply. You could probably squeeze all of them into a single freshman suite at Harvard. Even the most selective schools have to dip into the general pool of humanity to fill their freshman classes. You shouldn't discount your chances simply because you feel you don't measure up to admissions officers' ideals. There are many boring adults in this country, and many of them went to college. There are also many people who, no matter how boring they seem to their friends, seem terribly interesting to admissions officers.

At the same time—there's always a catch—the more closely you resemble the ideal candidate, the better your chances of admission will be.

WHY YOU NEED THIS BOOK

This book contains advice about every aspect of the admissions process, from taking the SAT to selecting a photo for your application. It tells you how to pick an appropriate college and how to go about finding financial aid. Most important, it gives you inside information that you'll never receive from anyone else.

If you're a high school junior or senior, you've probably already heard a lot of confusing advice about getting into college. Most of that confusing advice was probably offered with the very best of intentions. All the people who have ever been admitted to college—or whose kids have been admitted to college—consider themselves experts. Our experience is that there are very few experts.

THE PRINCETON REVIEW APPROACH

You may already know about The Princeton Review from our popular website www.princetonreview.com. Perhaps you've heard of us through someone who we've helped prepare for the SAT. Every year, we help over half of all college-bound students through our website, books, online courses, and live courses.

Our classes are small and are arranged according to ability. Every year, we spend hundreds of thousands of dollars writing, improving, and updating our course materials. Our teachers are sharp, enthusiastic people who have good SAT scores and recently graduated from top colleges. And our results are unmatched—our students raise their SAT scores by an average of 140 points.

In the twenty years since we started, The Princeton Review has become the most popular SAT preparation course in the country (and we're quickly becoming the most popular preparation course for the MCAT, LSAT, GMAT, and GRE).

Our techniques for doing better on standardized tests work because they are based on the same principles that the SAT's publisher uses to create the test. We help our students by teaching them how to think like the people who write the questions.

Our technique for getting into college works the same way. We can improve your admissions chances by teaching you how to think like the people who will be reading your application. When you understand how they think, you'll have a much easier time presenting yourself as the type of person they want to admit.

More importantly, we will also teach you how most *applicants* think. The task you face when you fill out a college application is to make yourself stand out from hundreds or thousands of other high school seniors who are in many ways exactly like you. The more you sound like everybody else, the less chance you'll have of catching an admissions officer's attention.

THE JOE BLOGGS PRINCIPLE

"Standing out" may sound like an obvious strategy, but you'd be surprised at how few applicants actually manage to do it. In fact, some candidates never sound *more* like everybody else than when they're trying hardest to sound *different*. The reason for this is that most of us, unless we're extremely careful, tend to think in very predictable ways.

Understanding this simple fact is one of the keys to the success of The Princeton Review's method for cracking the SAT. In our SAT courses, we teach our students about an imaginary test-taker named Joe Bloggs. Joe Bloggs is the average American high school student. He has average grades and average SAT scores. He isn't brilliant. He isn't stupid. He's exactly average.

On the SAT, Joe Bloggs thinks in a very predictable way. We can teach our students how to score higher simply by teaching them to avoid the traps that Joe Bloggs invariably falls into. By the end of our course, our students can spot and avoid "Joe Bloggs answers"—that is, answer choices that are very appealing but incorrect—from a mile away.

JOE BLOGGS ALSO APPLIES TO COLLEGE

When Joe Bloggs applies to college, he is just as predictable as he is when he takes the SAT. Since there's at least a little bit of Joe Bloggs in all of us, we all tend to sound a little bit like him—and consequently like everybody else—when we fill out our applications.

SO, DON'T BE A BLOGGS!

Much of the rest of this book is devoted to showing you, both directly and indirectly, how to conquer Joe Bloggs and make your application stand out and not be like his. The fewer "Joe Bloggs answers" you type on your application, the better your chances of being accepted at a selective school.

A SUBJECTIVE PROCESS

No matter how scientific and systematic your guidance counselor may sometimes sound, applying to college is a highly personal and subjective experience. Adults sometimes have trouble remembering exactly why they were initially attracted to the college they ended up happily attending. To be near the mountains? To be near a boyfriend? Because of something a parent said? Because of an advertisement in a magazine?

We can't give you a foolproof, step-by-step plan for getting into college. No one can. Even if you could be completely scientific about figuring out where you want to go and what you need to do to get in, your case would still be in the hands of extremely subjective admissions officers. No matter how rational *you* are, your fate could still end up being decided by a grumpy person whose car broke down that morning.

Since the admissions process is so subjective, for both applicants and admissions officers, we aren't going to offer you a hard-and-fast formula for acceptance. Such formulas just don't work. Our advice is less scientific, but more useful. We'll give you the kind of information you need to avoid the pitfalls that await the uninformed student. We'll give you insight into the minds of the people who will decide whether to admit or reject you.

We'll teach you how not to be Joe Bloggs.

DON'T GET CARRIED AWAY

Going to college is a big step for most people, but it isn't the most important thing in the world. There are many happy, successful people who never went to college. There are many unhappy, unsuccessful people with college degrees. Who you are inside is more important than where, or whether, you went to college.

If we sometimes sound as though we've forgotten that, it's only because we believe that if you do want to go to college, you have a right to know how the system really works. If your favorite extracurricular activity is one that we've observed to be unimpressive to admissions officers, that doesn't mean you should find something else to do after school. It simply means that you need to know how the admissions officers think. That's why we wrote this book.

HOW THIS BOOK IS ORGANIZED

There are two kinds of colleges: the ones you want to go to and the ones you can get into. With luck and a little planning, you'll find substantial overlap between the two categories.

The first chapter of this book is devoted to helping you think about where you want to go to college. This is a personal decision, of course, but we can make it easier for you by giving you information that students don't usually have and by helping you avoid some common pitfalls.

Most of the rest of the book is devoted to helping you maximize your chances of being accepted to the colleges that appeal to you. Separate sections or chapters are devoted to such important factors as test scores, interviews, application essays, and your high school record.

We suggest that you read the book straight through and then refer back to particular chapters as you need them.

IS IT TOO LATE? IS IT TOO EARLY?

Your parents may have begun thinking about where they wanted you to go to college on the day you were born or even sooner. You may not be entirely convinced that you need to think about it yet, or you may think about it all the time. When is the right time to think about going to college?

Well, senior year is a bit late. Application deadlines arrive quickly if you don't start writing to colleges before the first semester of twelfth grade. If you're already a senior and you haven't done anything yet, spend the rest of the afternoon reading this book and get cracking.

If you're a ninth or tenth grader, you're probably rushing things; although it's never too early to start taking tough courses and getting good grades. It's too early, however, to write away for applications from colleges. Don't sacrifice a complete high school experience for daydreams about college. Focus on making the most of high school. That said, you should consider looking through this book so that you know what to expect as you progress toward your senior year, and so that you don't do anything now that will mess up your chances later.

The best time to start thinking seriously about college is your junior year. By that time, you'll have a fairly good idea of what your high school grade point average and class rank are likely to be, and you'll have some test scores under your belt, too. With those pieces of information, you'll begin to develop an idea of the sort of schools to which you can realistically hope to be admitted.

WHO AM I, ANYWAY?

In writing this book, we have assumed that you are interested in attending a selective college. By "selective college" we mean a school that rejects significant numbers of applicants. This is common sense. If the college you want to attend accepts everyone who applies, you shouldn't need to read a book to tell you how to get in.

The advice in this book is generally geared toward the more selective of the selective schools—the 200 colleges in the country that are the hardest to get into. It also applies, with certain variations that we'll tell you about later, to state colleges and universities. Just remember that there are colleges with many different degrees of selectivity, and an applicant who is rejected by one school may be welcomed with open arms (and possibly offered a scholarship) by another.

If we sometimes seem to fall into the "perfect applicant" fallacy that we mentioned at the beginning of this introduction—by describing larger-than-life candidates who couldn't possibly exist—keep in mind that selectivity is a broad spectrum. Your task is to make yourself the best candidate you can be, given what you've been up to for the past three years. To begin tackling that task, read on.

CHAPTER ONE:
PICKING COLLEGES

Before you can be admitted to the college of your choice, you have to decide what the college of your choice is. Your decision will be influenced heavily by some factors over which you have no control—such as your parents' income and the grades you've already earned. It will also be influenced, perhaps decisively, by factors that are entirely personal. Most high school students change their minds many times. Some don't decide until the day their deposits are due.

IS THERE A SCIENTIFIC SYSTEM?

Many high school guidance counselors and how-to-get-into-college books recommend that students construct incredibly elaborate charts and tables ranking different schools according to such factors as size, location, curriculum, and atmosphere. School A wins so many points for having a home economics department, School B loses points for not allowing freshmen to park on campus.

If you're the type of person who makes many lists and enjoys ranking things on scales of one to ten, you'll undoubtedly make a chart comparing possible colleges. If you aren't such a person, you probably won't, and there's nothing that anyone could tell you that would make you more likely to do it. Our experience has been that students almost never make fancy charts like the ones in the guidance books. One of our students told us that she spent most of an afternoon making an elaborate filing system for college materials. She bought a cardboard file and filled it with folders and dividers. Then it sat. After a week, she was stuffing dirty clothes into it.

Furthermore, students who do make complicated charts seldom learn anything very meaningful from them. Unless you are intimately familiar with the schools you're considering, your evaluations of "atmosphere," "academic rigor," "class size," and so on won't mean very much. Does Oberlin deserve a five or an eight for "faculty advising programs?" Even Oberlin would have trouble answering that one. And even if you could answer it, what would your answer tell you? Just what sort of "faculty advising" do you think you're going to need?

SO WHAT DO I DO INSTEAD?

No one can make your college decision for you, and no one can tell you exactly how to go about making it. The purpose of this chapter is not to give you a step-by-step program for arriving at the "perfect" college choice, but rather to give you some important information that should help you clarify your thoughts. This is information that Princeton Review students have found useful over the years. It is not information that guidance counselors, parents, teachers, or admissions officers usually give.

HOW TO BEGIN

Most high school students have at least a few schools in mind as they begin to think about college. Your father wants you to go to Vanderbilt; your mother went to the University of Florida; your brother is at Occidental; someone once told you something nice about Bard; your guidance counselor thinks you ought to go to a junior college. You can start your selection process by thinking about these schools. If you don't want to go to Vanderbilt, you're going to have to come up with an explanation that will sound reasonable to your father. ("Dad, I'm just too dumb.") The good news is that in thinking about why you don't want to go to Vanderbilt, you will make many discoveries about where you do want to go.

You might want to pick up The Princeton Review's *The Best 357 Colleges*. In addition to giving you all the normal information (location, cost, and admissions requirements), this book gives you the results of a survey of over 100,000 students currently enrolled at the country's top colleges. These students gave us detailed information on a broad range of issues, such as quality of life, overall satisfaction, and professor/student interaction. Granted, it's 100,000 subjective opinions, but it's a start.

Another place to go, of course, is the Internet. By logging on to www.princetonreview.com and clicking on counselor-o-matic, you can get a list of schools that fit your profile and the categories that you've indicated are important to you. The results are extremely dependent on how you've answered the questions, so if you misrepresent yourself, you'll have a list of colleges appropriate for someone else. Of course, if you're not sure what you're looking for, you might not be sure how to answer some of the questions. Don't sweat it. You can do as many searches as you need based on different combinations of answers. Or you can simply leave some of the questions blank. Counselor-o-matic is not intended to tell you where you should apply. It's intended to help you discover some schools that might interest you and that also might accept you.

Don't worry if your search for the perfect college seems unsystematic, even haphazard. In the end, every decision about which college to attend is subjective.

TWO QUESTIONS, TWO POINTS

We have found that it is helpful to ask yourself two general questions about every school you want to consider:

1. Do I want to go to school here for four years?

2. Do I want to live here for four years?

Surprisingly, the second question often ends up being more important than the first. Many colleges offer a good education; only a few offer chalet living and skiing after class.

Most people are adept at developing a general picture of what particular colleges are like. Where they get into trouble is in the details that don't seem significant until after they enroll. Here we're going to give you some specific things to think about. These are by no means the only criteria that you should take into consideration in evaluating colleges. You already know that you should think about the school's general reputation and whether it appeals to you on a gut level. Below are some other factors that perhaps you haven't thought much about yet, or that you've thought a lot about, but shouldn't have.

EIGHTEEN FACTORS (IN NO PARTICULAR ORDER) THAT DO AND DON'T MATTER

1. Money

A lot of colleges cost a lot of money. If your parents aren't rich, the cost will make a big difference. Even when colleges say they don't pay attention to applicants' financial need in accepting and rejecting students, they really do (see Chapter Seven).

How much money your parents can afford to spend on college is going to affect not only where you go to school but also what your life is like once you get there. Do you mind juggling several outside jobs with your schoolwork? Do you mind graduating with a heavy debt? Do you mind going to a school where virtually all of the students have more money than you do? There's a lot of financial aid out there, but few scholarships pay the entire bill, and most have strings attached. One of the first things you have to do is sit down with your parents and talk fully and honestly about the bottom line.

2. Distance

When you're calculating college costs, don't forget to add in the cost of transportation. Flying back and forth between school and home can cost a few thousand dollars a year, particularly if school and home aren't located on heavily traveled discount air routes. Don't decide that you'll save money by staying at school during all your vacations. Students stranded on empty campuses during big holidays are among the most depressed people in the world. Some colleges even assign staff members to look after such students to ensure they don't throw themselves out of windows on Christmas Eve. Spending holidays away from home may sound like a great idea to you now, but a rough first semester as a freshman could change your mind.

3. Location

City or country? Can you stand four years of funny accents? Do you mind living on the fringes of a high-crime area? Do you mind not seeing first-run movies? Do you mind living in a town that has no good restaurants?

These questions have nothing to do with education, but they are not frivolous. Again, you're selecting not only a school but also a place to live. Be sure you want to live there before you sign up to go. Also remember that if you're going to have to work your way through school, a big city will offer more employment opportunities than a small town. It will also make it easier to find jobs that won't bring you into constant contact with your schoolmates, if that would bother you.

4. Climate

If you grew up in Florida, you're probably going to have trouble adjusting to winters in Maine. You're also going to have to buy a lot of new clothes. Weather can make a big difference in your state of mind. If rainy days make you feel gloomy, you may want to think twice about going to college in Oregon.

5. Living Arrangements

How you live is just as important as where you live. Colleges differ greatly in the housing they offer. Some offer none at all. Some don't permit off-campus living. Do you mind showering in front of a dozen other people? Are single rooms available for freshmen? If it matters to you, find out.

It may sound silly, but things like the location of freshman dormitories can make a bigger impression on a freshman's mind than the quality of freshman courses. Your living arrangements will influence who your friends are, how you spend your free time, how early you have to get up in the morning, and how late you can stay out at night.

Here's how one of our former students puts it: "The best thing about college for me isn't college, it's my apartment. After freshman year, you're allowed to live off campus. My parents give me what they would have spent on room and board, and I use it to pay my rent and buy my food. I sleep in a bed I bought for ten dollars, I make my own breakfast and my own coffee, and when school's over for the day I drink a beer in my own living room. I feel like an adult. And my grades are better too."

That's just the way one student thinks about it. You might be a lot happier living in a dormitory around other students. But this particular student's college experience would have been a lot different if he had attended a school that didn't let sophomores live off campus. You can't anticipate exactly how you'll feel about this sort of thing, but by now you know enough about your likes and dislikes to have a reasonably good idea of how you might like to live.

Life in virtually all freshman dormitories is alike in some respects: It's loud, messy, crowded, uncomfortable, and usually a lot of fun. There are important differences, though, and understanding them before you make a commitment can lead to a happier few years.

6. Where Your Friends Go

Going to college with high school friends can be great or terrible, depending. On the one hand, going away to a college where you don't know anybody is one of the few opportunities you'll have in life to wipe the slate clean on the person you used to be. Even better, it comes at a time when many people are very eager to wipe the slate clean. If you don't know anybody on campus, no one will know about the time the captain of the football team hung you from a coat hook by the band of your underpants. On the other hand, having a close friend nearby can make the first weeks of freshman year less frightening.

Nevertheless, we feel you're probably better off on your own. You'll make more new friends if you don't have the old gang to fall back on. Feelings of freshman alienation usually don't last beyond the first couple of weeks. People also change at college. The kind of people you like to hang around with won't necessarily stay the same.

7. Where Your Girlfriend or Boyfriend Goes

A fair number of people marry their high school sweethearts, but many more of them don't. Before you decide to attend a certain college to be with your current boyfriend or girlfriend, think through the consequences.

Freshman year in college can put a huge strain on a high school romance. Dormitory life is fun and liberating. Even small colleges offer temptations that high schools don't. It takes a strong relationship to survive the dramatic change in lifestyle that freshman year in college means to most people. We knew two students who had been going steady since eighth grade. They ordered catalogs together, picked colleges together, filled out their applications together, and enrolled in the same school. Then, a week into freshman year, they broke up. They spent most of the first semester just trying to avoid each other on campus, which was hard because they were at a small school. He ended up transferring.

Having a steady boyfriend or girlfriend nearby can limit your ability to make new friends of both sexes. If you spend all your time with your high school sweetheart, you're not going to meet a lot of other people. Many people's fondest memories of freshman year involve informal group activities in which no clear couples were differentiated.

Adults tend to say that if a relationship is meant to last, it will last. This isn't necessarily true, but a strong relationship will survive some distance. Our advice is to attend college a few hours away from each other.

8. Trends

Every year a few hot schools emerge to which everyone seems to apply. Hot schools are usually good colleges that are suddenly perceived as being easier to get into than the very best colleges or are schools that have suddenly seen an increase in national exposure and attention. As a result, they attract a huge number of applications and sometimes actually become harder to get into than other schools that are perceived as better.

Recently, New York University, Boston University, and Penn State University, to name a few, have been very hot.

Remember what we said about Joe Bloggs. When Joe Bloggs hears about a hot school, his reaction is, "Hey I'd better apply too!" But the more people who want to go to a school, the more people who are going to be rejected. The movie that has the longest line of people waiting to see it may be a great movie, but it won't matter if you can't get a seat.

This doesn't mean you shouldn't apply to a hot school. It just means you shouldn't depend on getting in, even if your credentials would ordinarily make you a strong contender. Pay attention to the colleges your classmates are applying to and use your judgment. If you decide to apply to a certain school because you read an interesting article about it in *Time,* remember that several million other people will have read about it too.

9. Student/Faculty Ratio and Average Class Size

If it's possible to deduce anything important from a student/faculty ratio, we don't know what it is. Don't worry about it. Many colleges fudge their statistics anyway.

Much the same can be said for average class size, another statistic to which applicants pay too much attention. Course quality is much more important than class size (although it's also much harder to assess, unfortunately). Huge courses taught by great teachers are more rewarding than tiny courses taught by morons. In small classes, you often have to spend an excessive amount of time listening to the opinions of your classmates. Some professors who shine in big lecture courses are unbearable in small seminars.

One of our students summed it up for us nicely: "I came from a big high school where there were never enough desks, and one of the things I cared about most when I applied to college was class size—I wanted them small. But the funny thing was [that] my very worst class freshman year was an English class that only had six students in it and that usually met in the professor's living room. The professor was a creep, and the students were creeps, and there was nowhere to hide. And my favorite course was a freshman science course that met in an auditorium and had about 500 students in it. The professor was like a great actor, and every lecture was exciting."

Also remember that student/faculty ratio and average class size mean even less if the courses you plan to take don't fit the usual pattern. If you are planning to major in Greek and the university to which you're applying only has seven Greek majors, many of your classes are going to be small no matter what the overall university statistics say.

10. Course Catalogs

Some students try to compare colleges on the basis of catalogs of course offerings. As college freshmen soon discover, though, course catalogs are works of fiction. Courses that sound great on the printed page are often hideous in reality. The course that makes you want to go to Antioch may be canceled by the time you get there. Who the teacher is usually makes more difference than what is being taught, and it's almost impossible to evaluate the teachers until you're actually on campus and taking their courses.

Of course, if you have special academic interests, you need to be certain that the colleges you are considering can satisfy them. If you want to major in Russian, be sure the schools you apply to have Russian departments. Remember, many students don't stay with the majors they start out with, but if you are interested in exploring some possible majors, you might want to take a look at The Princeton Review's *Guide to College Majors*. The book includes great information about majors and careers, but it doesn't include a list of schools that offer each major. For that, you should go to www.princetonreview.com, click on "research," and then "find a major." You can view every school that offers the majors that interest you.

11. Faculty Credentials

You may very well have been told that a good way to compare colleges is to look in the back of course catalogs to see how many professors have PhDs. Don't bother. The catalogs don't provide nearly enough information about faculty members for you to make meaningful comparisons. The general prestige of a college will give you some idea of the quality of the faculty, but lists of where professors went to school and what degrees they earned won't help you. Nor will average age, percentage of tenured professors, or any other sweeping statistic that doesn't take the individual into account.

12. Viewbooks

Many colleges supplement their catalogs with viewbooks, brochures, and other publications. You can get some idea of what a campus is like by looking at the pictures, but no college in existence looks as good as it does in its viewbook. A viewbook is an advertisement. The college hopes that it will put you in the mood to buy. Four magnificent years in downtown Los Angeles for just $100,000! You should be just as skeptical of a viewbook as you are of the claims in a television commercial. You will never find a college that has the same proportion of happy students, magnificent scenery, and beautiful weather that it depicts in its brochures.

Colleges also use their viewbooks to spell out their educational philosophies. Most colleges have interchangeable philosophies—"a firm commitment to the liberal arts," and so on—but some colleges do have unusual programs or other specialized approaches to education. These will always be explained in the viewbook or other brochure. Dartmouth, for instance, requires that during one year you spend a summer on campus instead of a winter. Drew University has a program that allows every undergrad to take a January term for five weeks in a foreign country. Northeastern has a five-year co-op program, and NYU, Boston University, Temple, and Wagner, to name just a few, have expanded Experiential Learning Programs that expose first- and second-year students to outside-of-the-classroom course work.

Bottom line: when you look at viewbooks, focus on the programs, not just the pictures.

13. What Your Parents Think

Unless you're still earning residuals from those peanut butter commercials you did as a child, you're probably going to need your parents' help in financing your education. Don't alienate them by telling them right off the bat that you don't care what they think. As of this writing, college tuition is not tax deductible—in other words, your parents will have to earn $150,000 to be able to send you to a private college (by the way, you are an only child, aren't you?). If you want to go to an Ivy League university and they want to economize by sending you to the local community college, appeal to their vanity. Try persuading them at least to let you apply. If you get in, your case will be strengthened; if you don't, there's nothing to fight about.

A mistake many high school students make is letting their parents' wishes prevent them from applying to schools they would actually enjoy attending. Don't refuse to apply to a particular college just because your mother wants you to go there. Think these things out rationally. Think about what *you* want. If there's substantial overlap between what you want and what your parents want, so be it. Also, do your homework. If money is the problem, find out about sources of financial aid before you talk to your parents (see Chapter Seven).

Remember that many students change their minds often about where they want to go to college. If you are determined to do battle with your parents, make sure you're fighting over a school that genuinely means something to you. If you fight with your parents and win, you may find it difficult to back down later. Are you that set on going to school three thousand miles from home?

14. What Your Guidance Counselor Thinks
Most counselors are knowledgeable and really do care. Listen to what they have to say. On the other hand, many counselors are overworked (in a budget crunch, the counselors are among

the first to go), and some are just bad. A counselor may have to advise hundreds of students about personal, career, and academic concerns, not to mention college planning. Moreover, even the best counselor cannot be expected to know about all of the programs and departments at the colleges around the country.

If you are applying to a college or program outside your counselor's experience, you'll have to do some research on your own. If you feel you cannot talk to your counselor because he or she is overworked, you should consider seeking the help of a good independent college adviser.

Here are a few things to watch out for—

- Does your guidance counselor know you by sight? Is he or she familiar with the courses and extracurricular activities you're taking? Remember: Counselors cannot read minds. It's your job to let your counselor know all your activities, achievements, and goals. Admissions officers are unimpressed by letters of recommendation written by counselors who obviously don't know the students they're recommending.

- Does your high school regularly send graduates to colleges equal in caliber to the ones you want to attend? If not, your counselor may not be much help in advising you.

- How many students is your counselor handling? If he or she has 500 students, don't expect that much personal attention. According to Alan McLeod, one of the top counselors in New York, counselors should be working with no more than fifty students at a time.

- Are the publications in your counselor's office extensive and up to date? Only the most recent brochures provide reliable information.

- Is your counselor knowledgeable about SAT and ACT testing dates, registration procedures, and so on? Most counselors are, but if yours is not, you're going to have to be responsible about getting this information yourself. You can get registration information about the SAT at www.collegeboard.com and about the ACT at www.act.org.

- Does your counselor tend to recommend the same few schools again and again to you and your classmates? Did he tell the smartest kid in your class to apply to colleges you've never heard of? Some counselors act as though there were only three or four colleges in the country. Beware. Dr.

John S. Yaegel, former president of the New Jersey School Counselor Association, says to be sure you ask your counselor to investigate a wide scope of challenging colleges with you, including some "safeties" where you know you'll be admitted.

15. SAT/ACT Averages

One of the first things students do when they begin to think about college is to look up colleges in a college guide (such as the College Board's *College Handbook* or our own *The Best 357 Colleges*) or on the Internet, and then eliminate schools whose average SAT or ACT score is higher than their own test scores. This can be dangerous, for a number of complicated and sometimes contradictory reasons.

- An average is an average, not a cutoff. If a college's average verbal SAT is 550, that means that half of the students scored below 550.

- Colleges lie about their SAT averages. The colleges themselves supply the numbers printed in the directories, and sometimes they exaggerate. All colleges want to look selective. Sometimes they do that by inflating their averages. They may do it by giving the average scores of the students they admit rather than of those who enroll. (A school can inflate its average by admitting a lot of high-scoring students it knows will probably end up going somewhere else.) They may also do it by using only their students' best scores. They may do it by eliminating the scores of minorities or athletes, who as a group do worse on admissions tests than others do, from the totals.

- Schools' fibbing about SAT averages can work both for you and against you. On the one hand, a school may be easier to get into than its claimed average may seem to suggest. On the other hand, a school may be so worried about its SAT average that it avoids students with lower-than-average scores.

- Some colleges are actually harder to get into than their published SAT averages suggest. If an average includes the scores of minority students (which, as we said, tend to be lower), the effective cutoff for non-minority students will be higher than it seems to be. We'll tell you more about this in Chapter Six.

- SAT scores are often evaluated on a scale along with GPA or class rank. If your SAT score is below a college's average but your

GPA and class rank are above that sam
college's average, you'll be evaluated dif
ferently than if both your SAT and your GPA
are below that college's average.

- If you've only taken the PSAT, comparing
  your scores with SAT averages will probably be misleading. Most students' scores go
  up when they take the SAT. (see Chapter
  Two.) Our advice is to look at the SAT averages in the guides, but to use a wide net.
  Any school whose SAT average is within
  200 points of your own composite should
  pass this test.

16. School Size

The size of the college you attend can have a big effect on your
experience there. Big schools have more activities, more facili-
ties, more students, more everything. It's easier to stand out at
a small school, but harder to melt into the crowd. At a big
school you have to take a greater responsibility for planning
your own education and securing your own living arrangements
than you do at a small school.

You shouldn't have any trouble thinking of plenty of differences between big and small schools. Think of the differences
between living in a town and living in a city.

But some differences between large and small schools are
exaggerated. For example, many high school students say that
they don't want to go to a small school because they won't be

ble to "meet enough people." Now, let's be serious. How many people do you know now? How many do you think you'll meet at a university with 50,000 students? In fact, students often meet more people at smaller schools than they do at big ones, simply because the overall environment isn't as intimidating. On the other hand, big schools are usually broken down into smaller units. Even though you attend a huge university, you may spend virtually all of your time with the fewer than 4,000 students in the undergraduate college of arts and sciences.

Size is important, but it's sometimes not as important as most high school students tend to think it is. Stop thinking like most high school students!

17. Library Size

The number of volumes in a college's library can make a difference, but think about this carefully. It is not unknown for a high school student to cross a college off his list because its library is "too small," then go to a college with a bigger library and not set foot inside it during four years except to use the bathroom. For most students, computer labs and Internet access are far more important than the number of volumes in the library.

18. Computer/Internet Access

Computer labs are often located in residence halls and libraries and are sometimes open 24 hours a day. "Hot spots" for free Internet access cover the grounds of many campuses. Increasingly, professors post syllabi, assignments, and additional reading materials online, and internal college websites allow you to schedule classes and apply for financial aid efficiently and securely. Still, even though virtually all colleges have integrated technology into the college experience, they have done so to varying degrees. Some colleges expect you to use technology daily. Others make it available but don't necessarily expect you to use it, other than to write your papers.

The best people to ask about the use of technology at a college are the students at that college. If you're comfortable asking them on a college visit, most students will have well-developed opinions regarding everything from how easy it is to access a printer on campus to how annoying the college's internal website is.

WHERE DO I GO TO FIND OUT ABOUT COLLEGES?

Many sources of information about particular colleges are available to you. (In fact, there are too many.) Here are some of the most important ones and what we think of them

1. Visits

There are two kinds of college trips, and you may benefit from both.

The first kind is a trip with your parents, usually taken during the summer between your junior and senior years. Frankly, you're not going to learn a lot about the colleges (for one thing, most of the schools you visit won't be in session), but it's a good chance to get to know your folks better and share your thoughts about college.

The second kind of trip is usually more helpful. This is a trip you take with a friend during the fall of your senior year. You may even have an older friend or a sibling already enrolled at a college you think you might want to attend. (If you don't know anyone on campus, the admissions office will often arrange for you to stay with students.) Hang around in the student union, visit some classes, buy a sweatshirt at the bookstore, and try to get the feel of the place.

Many counselors and how-to-get-into-college books recommend that you strike up conversations with passing students and ask them what they think of their school. If you feel comfortable talking to strangers, go ahead. If you feel a little squeamish about walking up to a student on the street, try going to the campus cafeteria instead. Just sit down at a table with a few other people and let the conversation come naturally. And even if it doesn't come naturally and you don't end up talking at length with some of the kids, don't sweat it—hanging around and checking things out can be just as valuable. By the way, don't worry that everyone will know you're a high school student. They won't.

Visits to nearby colleges are often less intimidating and easier to arrange than treks to distant parts of the country. Be sure to leave your parents at home. Most admissions offices arrange campus tours, often conducted by students. If you're interested in joining one of these, call ahead.

When you visit colleges, be careful that you don't let yourself be swayed by factors that don't really matter. Don't decide to go to a school just because someone smiled at you on the steps of the library. And don't decide not to go there just because it was cold and rainy on the day of your visit.

Many colleges offer, and some colleges strongly suggest, on-campus interviews. If so, a trip may be even more helpful or necessary. We'll tell you more about these interviews in Chapter Four.

If you're thinking about visiting several schools, it might be a good idea to look at The Princeton Review's *Visiting College Campuses*. It'll help you plan your trip to 250 selective colleges, and give you advice on where to get a hotel and when to go.

2. College Representatives

Many admissions officers spend a lot of time traveling around the country and talking with high school students. If a college is popular with students at your high school, an admissions officer may schedule a meeting right at your school. Other admissions officers conduct regional information sessions or take part in college fairs.

These meetings are sometimes more useful to colleges than they are to high school students. Colleges use them to promote themselves and attract applications. You can pick up information at these meetings, but you should always keep in mind that the colleges are trying to sell you something.

You should also keep in mind that the impression you make at these meetings can have a bearing on your chances for admission. You will probably be asked to sign your name in a book or fill out an information card when you arrive. If you make a bad impression (because you didn't wear shoes and asked a stupid question), the admissions officer conducting the meeting may remember you. Admissions officers often take notes on the meetings they conduct, sometimes making notations directly on the information cards filled out by the students. (They do this even when they say they don't.)

It would be a mistake to try to stand out at one of these meetings: Don't try to monopolize the admissions officer's attention and certainly don't brag about your SAT scores. The most important thing is not to make an indelibly bad impression. You don't want to start the admissions process with a strike against you.

3. The Colleges Themselves, by Mail and by Website

Earlier in this chapter, we told you not to pay too much attention to the rosy pictures colleges present of themselves in their viewbooks, brochures, and on their websites. Even so, you can glean some important information from these sources. They will tell you about living arrangements, academic and other requirements (both for admission and for graduation), special programs, costs, financial aid opportunities and procedures, and other factors that will influence your decision.

You can receive viewbooks and brochures simply by e-mailing or writing the colleges to which you are interested in applying. You should do this no later than the summer before your senior year (and no earlier than the spring of your junior year). Don't write a letter containing your life history. Just send an e-mail to the admissions office requesting information about the school and an application. Keep it brief, but don't forget your name and address. Alternatively, you can send a postcard. Again, there's no need to be fancy. Just request information and they'll send it to you.

No college is going to admit or reject you on the basis of your request for an application, but at the same time, a good impression is worth giving. Whether by e-mail or postcard, all of your communications with colleges should be free of spelling or grammatical errors, and should be neat, respectful, and concise.

Colleges respond to requests for information and applications in many different ways. Some will send you an application immediately, or will e-mail you to advise you to fill out an application online. Others will send you a letter or e-mail explaining that a catalog and other materials are being mailed to you separately. Others will send a preliminary application or an e-mail requesting a few additional pieces of information, such as your full name and the name of your high school. Most will write to you more than once. When you're on a school's distribution list, you can expect to stay on it for quite a while. Keep track of all this stuff, and keep the hard copies of applications in a separate file or drawer so they won't get banged around.

4. Guides, Directories, and Online Search Engines

Reading the big directories like *The College Handbook* is a little like reading the phone book. You have to pick through a lot of information you'll never need. It's best to try to get a guide that focuses on selective and highly selective colleges, and guides that give you the perspective of students. Of course, as we've mentioned before, our own *The Best 357 Colleges* includes results from surveys of over 100,000 students at over 300 schools that give you the real scoop on our country's revered academic institutions. Whatever guide you choose, remember to use it as a starting point to help you find some colleges that you're interested in, not as a way of finding the one and only college that is best for you. Once you've found some colleges you're interested in, you can investigate them further on the Internet and, most importantly, through visits.

One way to help you focus your attention on schools that match your qualifications and interests is to use an online search engine. Earlier in this chapter, we mentioned counselor-o-matic, which you can access at www.princetonreview.com. By using a search engine, you can quickly find schools that match your criteria. If the search gives you some schools that you think you might be interested in, you can then investigate those schools further through visits, college representatives, and college publications.

WHAT? ME? WORRY?

It's important to remember that most students end up liking where they go to college. The student who is crushed to have been rejected by Princeton ends up loving Oberlin and even being happy that the Fates kept her from being accepted by what had once been her first choice. In many ways, the most important thing about college is the one characteristic that virtually all colleges have in common: They are communities of young people living on their own without many serious responsibilities. You'll never get another chance to do it, and you'll probably enjoy it almost anywhere you have a chance.

Where you go to college can be very important. In addition to determining where you spend the next four years of your life, where you go to school can determine where you work after graduation, whom you marry, where you live, and who your lifelong friends are. A degree from Wharton really can make it easier to get a good job after graduation; however, spending four years in a glamorous state like Colorado or Hawaii really can be a lot of fun. You should make your college decision carefully and with a clear head. Don't make your decision simply to please (or infuriate) someone else.

If you begin to think that you won't be able to go on living unless you get into (let's say) Yale, get a hold of Yale's faculty directory and see where its professors went to college. You'll see that some of them went to Yale, some to Harvard, some to other Ivy League schools, but many of them went to exactly the sort of colleges that you think are beneath you. If those colleges are good enough for Yale, might they not also be good enough for you? You should approach college selection thoughtfully, but not with a conviction that your entire life hangs in the balance.

QUESTIONS AND ANSWERS

How many colleges should I apply to?

Six.

Actually, we just made that up. But six is probably a pretty good number. If you apply to more than that, you'll have to devote your life to it. Besides, nobody needs more than six choices.

Be certain that one of the schools you apply to is a school you are absolutely positive you'll be admitted to—a safety school. (Also be certain that your safety school is a school you wouldn't mind attending if you had to. Stranger things have happened.)

Even if you are absolutely positive that only two colleges exist that you could conceivably bear to attend, apply to a few more as well. You could change your mind later on.

Who makes admissions decisions?

Different colleges have different systems. At some, undergraduates and faculty members play a role. At others, all decisions are made by a small handful of professionals. At still others, decisions are made democratically by large committees.

Here's the way the admissions process works at one top Ivy League school: Students' applications are given a preliminary reading and assigned two ratings, personal and academic. Each is scored on a scale of 1 to 4, with 1 being the best. The academic rating is based on, in equal parts, grades and standardized test scores. The personal rating is based on extracurricular activities, interviews, and recommendations. If the combined rating is 4 or less, the student is assigned a "likely"; 6 or more is an "unlikely"; 5 is a "possible."

Even if you know the exact composition of the admissions office at a school to which you are applying, that knowledge won't do you much good. More important than who they are is what they are: tired of reading boring applications.

HOW HARD IS IT TO TRANSFER?

Generally speaking, the more prestigious a school is, the harder it is to transfer into. The reason for this isn't difficult to understand: There just aren't a lot of students who leave schools like Harvard and Yale, and if they don't leave there isn't room for transfers. The easiest schools to transfer into are the ones with high attrition rates—but then you have to ask yourself, why are all those other students leaving?

Transferring isn't impossible, though. In fact, many colleges have found that transfer students do unusually well. A few rules apply

- Schools almost never accept transfer students who have completed more than two years in another college.

- Your college transcript will be the most important part of your application folder. SAT scores are used to predict college grades; once you have college grades, the scores are less important.

- Colleges typically do require test scores for transfer students, though. Most transfer applicants simply submit the scores they received in high school. We recommend, however, that you take the test again. You'll almost certainly score higher than you did in high school.

- Colleges don't make transfer decisions until after they've filled the freshman class. This means you probably won't hear whether you've been admitted until the summer, even the late summer. Be sure you have a contingency plan ready if you get turned down.

- Colleges usually expect transfer applicants to have clear, compelling academic reasons for wanting to switch schools. Simply being unhappy at your present school isn't enough. The best reason is a strong desire to pursue a course of study that isn't offered at your present school. You'll have to make your case in detail, and you'll have to be convincing. A transfer applicant, unlike a freshman applicant, can't get away with being "undecided" about academic goals.

- Your application has to make sense. It is virtually impossible to transfer to Harvard from Princeton or Yale, for example. Harvard's admissions office will decide, justifiably, that you are attending a very good school right now and that you don't need to be rescued.

WHAT IS A WAITING LIST?

All selective colleges admit more students than they have room for. They do this because they know that many of the students they admit won't actually enroll. Guessing how many students will enroll is a very inexact science. To protect themselves, most colleges have waiting lists. An applicant who is "wait-listed" is one who may be admitted if enough students decide to go somewhere else.

If you're wait-listed at a school you want to attend, you can usually help your case substantially. Write a letter reaffirming your desire to attend the school. Ask your guidance counselor to call the admissions office. Send a letter describing any honors you've won since you sent in your application. If you have a connection, pull it. When colleges admit students from waiting lists, they almost always give preference to students who have made it clear they really want to attend.

At the very most popular and selective schools, admissions from waiting lists are sometimes few and far between. Your guidance counselor can get a feel for your chances by making a phone call. Don't knock yourself out if the situation is hopeless, but remember that the places that do open up usually go to the students who make themselves heard.

My parents want to hire an independent counselor to advise me. Is this a good idea?

Independent guidance counselors are becoming quite popular, particularly in areas (such as New York City) with high concentrations of competitive high schools and anxious parents. The fees charged by these counselors can be very high—sometimes more than two thousand dollars. Some parents believe, though, that no expense is too great if it will give their children an edge.

Many bad independent counselors are out there (everybody's an expert, as you've probably already discovered). We heard of one man who claimed to have a friend on the admissions committee at Brown and offered a money-back guarantee of acceptance in return for a thousand dollars. This person did nothing but collect checks. Some of his "advisees" got in; most didn't. He returned the money of those who were rejected and pocketed the rest.

Some of the best independent counselors we know are former admissions officers from top selective colleges or former guidance counselors from first-rate high schools. These people can be very, very helpful. They can show you how to present your case in the best possible light, and they can give you good advice about which schools you should be considering.

Don't expect an independent counselor to pull strings for you. In fact, you shouldn't let an independent counselor write a recommendation for you or contact a school on your behalf. Most selective colleges don't like independent counselors, and students who have them can seem pushy. If you hire an independent, keep it to yourself. Listen to what he or she has to say, but don't let colleges know you have a paid helper.

Stay away from any independent counselor who promises to write your essay for you. That's cheating. You should expect a counselor to help you polish your essay, though, and to help you with grammar, spelling, and the appropriateness of your topic.

DELAYING AND DEFERRING COLLEGE

You (or maybe one of your parents) bought this book because you're going to college in a year or two. Everyone you know expects you to go to college. Your parents expect it, your buddies expect it, and I guess we do too, since we've written this book to help you get in. But are you sure you really want to go?

You have many choices about what to do next year, and college is only one of them. Not everybody is ready to go to college by the end of his senior year. Maybe you worked hard in high school and want some time to yourself. Maybe you want to work on your basic skills before embarking on the rigors of college. Maybe you skipped a grade at one point and feel you're too young. Hey—maybe you're just sick of school. Whatever the reason, if you go to college when you're not ready it can be a costly mistake.

If you think you need some skills, or some experience living away from home, look into a post-grad year of high school. Many prep schools offer them. Prep school courses give you more of a chance to catch up academically than college remedial courses do. A post-grad year offers you a chance to improve your record, straighten out your life, and apply to colleges as a much stronger candidate (assuming that you do the work). Junior colleges offer the same advantages: a chance to show colleges that you have changed for the better and can handle their workload.

Joining the military for a few years is another possibility. Not only will you pick up a few years' experience and gain valuable skills, but you will have a lot of financial help when you finally go to college (see Chapter Seven).

Then again, maybe you want to take a year off entirely, perhaps to see something of the world or to get work experience. If you are not sure why you are going to college, staying away for a year gives you some time to think things over, and to see what else is out there. If you think you might be interested in this option, you might want to take a look at *Taking Time Off,* our book that profiles twenty-six students who took time off and used it productively.

Of course, taking a year off has its downside, too. You fall a year behind your classmates. You could wind up wasting the entire year (but then, you might have wasted your first year at college, too). Applying next year may be a hassle, especially if you don't take care of all the red tape senior year. If you don't, you will have to track down old teachers to write recommendations and have to take standardized tests a year after you stop going to classes.

So if you plan to take next year off, we strongly recommend that you apply to college now, and defer the starting date only after you're admitted. Take your tests, collect your recommendations, and explore your college choices now. Almost all colleges will allow you to defer if you write them with your reasons and give them proper notice (usually by May 1).

Colleges send out their decisions on April 14. If you are accepted to the college of your choice, you can use the last two weeks of April to decide whether or not you want to defer for a year. You'd be surprised how much an acceptance can change your thinking! If you don't get in anywhere, you can always reapply next year—even to the same schools (colleges admire tenacity).

We want you to go to college. You'll like it. You'll learn a lot. You'll develop social skills. When you're not studying hard it's a blast. But not everyone goes to college immediately. Don't feel pressured into it. Four years in college is too much time, too much effort, and too much money for you to be anything less than enthusiastic about going.

CHAPTER TWO: TEST SCORES

If you stood on a street corner and asked people to say the first thing that popped into their minds when you said "applying to college," many of them would probably answer, "SAT scores!" The SAT, sponsored by the College Entrance Examination Board (College Board) and published by the Educational Testing Service (ETS), symbolizes the entire admissions process for many people. The same is true, to a lesser extent, of the ACT, a college admissions test published by a company called the American College Testing Program. We're going to spend most of our time in this chapter talking about the SAT, which is taken annually by over 2 million students, and which will soon undergo a major overhaul. We'll tell you more about the ACT later, and also about SAT II Subject Tests.

How important is the SAT? The answer to this question is complex. Unfortunately, most people treat the question as though it were simple. As a result, most of the information available about these tests is inaccurate. Much of the advice given to students about them is actually wrong.

HERE'S AN EXAMPLE OF WHAT WE MEAN

It's College Night at your high school, and you and your parents are attending a question-and-answer session with an admissions officer from an Ivy League university that you want to attend. Your mother raises her hand and asks if a student's SAT scores are the most important part of the application.

"The importance of the SAT in college admissions is greatly exaggerated," says the admissions officer. "It's one factor—*one* factor. It's not the most important factor; it's not even the *second* most important factor. I wish our applicants would spend more time worrying about their schoolwork and less time worrying about their scores on multiple-choice tests."

This sounds reasonable and reassuring. Your mother thinks, "Good, his scores don't matter." You think, "Great, I can blow off the test." Your school's guidance counselor thinks, "Wonderful, I can tell my students not to worry so much about the SAT."

But the very next day, the admissions officer goes back to his campus and resumes wading through applications.

"What do you think of X?" asks one of his colleagues, referring to a candidate they're considering.

"Good scores, nice grades. The SAT IIs jump around, though."

They discuss some other cases.

"That low verbal worries me."

"His grades are good, but the SATs are so much better I wonder if he's lazy."

"Good grades, mediocre scores—a classic overachiever."

And so on. The admissions officer wasn't lying on College Night when he said he thought the SAT was overemphasized. He just didn't realize that he was one of the people who overemphasized it.

SAT MYTHOLOGY

The story about the admissions officer illustrates an extremely important fact about standardized admissions tests: What people say about the tests very often bears little resemblance to reality. Even at schools that claim not to pay much attention to SAT scores, test scores are a constant topic of conversation.

Many myths have arisen about the SAT and similar tests. If you want to be a successful college candidate, you're going to have to learn to untangle fact from fiction.

WHAT, EXACTLY, IS THE SAT?

During 2004 and 2005, that's a confusing question to answer, because it's actually two different tests depending on when you take it.

Through January 2005, the SAT will continue to have the following components:

- Two Verbal Sections (30 minutes each), which include Sentence Completions, Analogies, and Reading Comprehension.

- One Verbal Section (15 minutes), which includes only Reading Comprehension questions.

- One regular Math Section (30 minutes), which includes arithmetic, algebra, and geometry questions in a standard five-answer, multiple-choice format.

- One strange Math Section (30 minutes), which includes fifteen questions that ask you compare data in two columns (Quantatative Comparision) and ten questions that require you to write in your answers rather than choose from five answer choices (Grid-ins).

- One short Math Section (15 minutes), which is just like the 30-minute regular math section.

- An Experimental Section, which doesn't count toward your score, and will either be a 30-minute Math Section or a 30-minute Verbal Section.

Beginning in March 2005, the test will change. If you're in the class of 2006 or later, you'll be expected to take the new SAT, which will have the following components:

- Two 25-minute Math Sections and one 20-minute Math Section. Quantitative Comparisons will be dropped. Some more advanced algebra II concepts will be added.

- Three Critical Reading Sections (formerly known as "Verbal"). Two sections will be 25 minutes, and one section will be 20 minutes. Analogies will be dropped. Most of the reading comprehension passages will be shorter.

- Two Writing Sections. One section will be a multiple-choice grammar section, similar to the Writing Section on the current PSAT, that asks you to improve sentences, paragraphs, or passages. The other section will require you to write a short essay, similar to the SAT II Writing Exam.

WHERE CAN I GET THE LATEST INFORMATION ON THE CHANGES?

The best way to keep on top of the changes is to log on to www.princetonreview.com. You can look at some sample questions and get updated advice regarding the new SAT.

WHERE DOES THE SAT COME FROM?

The SAT is published by ETS under the sponsorship of the College Board. ETS and the College Board are not government agencies, as many people believe. They do not have any connection with Princeton University, as many other people believe. They are private companies that make money by selling tests. ETS sells not only the SAT but also about 500 other tests, including ones for CIA agents, golf pros, travel agents, firefighters, and barbers.

WHO WRITES THE SAT?

Many people believe that SAT questions are written by famous college professors or experts on secondary education. This is not true. Virtually all questions are written by ordinary company employees or by college students and others hired part-time from outside ETS. Sometimes the questions are even written by teenagers. The daughter of an ETS vice president spent the summer after she graduated from high school writing questions for ETS tests.

WHAT DOES THE SAT MEASURE?

Each subject area of the exam is scored on a scale from 200 to 800, with the national average somewhere near 500. Very few students score above a 700 or below a 300.

If you're like most high school students, you think of the SAT as a test of how smart you are. If you score 800 on Math you'll probably think of yourself as a "genius"; if you score 200 you may think of yourself as an "idiot." You may even think of an SAT score as a permanent label, like your social security number.

Students sometimes come to us depressed about their PSAT and SAT scores. They'd always thought of themselves as reasonably smart; now they're bummed because ETS has branded them as "stupid." Their entire self-image has been deflated by a number on a piece of paper.

This shouldn't happen. The SAT isn't a test of how smart you are. It's simply a test of how good you are at taking ETS tests. Princeton Review students improve their SAT scores by an *average* of 140 points on the two halves (Math and Verbal) of the test combined. (We'll tell you more about improving your SAT scores later.) Our students aren't any *smarter* when they finish taking our course; they're just better at taking the SAT.

We teach our students not to be intimidated by the SAT. When they leave us, they think of the SAT as a game, not a life-or-death test. They no longer brag about high scores or have nightmares about low ones. They see the test for what it is: a bad joke played on more than two million kids a year by a bunch of bureaucrats in New Jersey.

WHAT DO ADMISSIONS OFFICERS THINK ABOUT THE SAT?

No matter what they say on College Night, virtually all admissions officers think of the SAT as a test of how "smart" you are. They may believe that the test is flawed, they may believe that there are better measures of preparation for college (there are)—but they still think of the SAT as a measure of your intelligence. If you are an A student but have mediocre SAT scores, they'll call you an "overachiever," not an "under-tester." Even college admissions officers who claim not to believe in the SAT have a powerful tendency to believe SAT scores when they see them. This tendency isn't based on past experience with real students; it's based on a nearly universal tendency to believe that numbers—any numbers—are "real" and "scientific." When admissions officers juggle numbers around, they feel that they're making objective decisions. The scores are a powerful crutch. An admissions officer once told us, "I need the numbers, and I don't care where they come from." He said he was joking—but he wasn't completely.

Some admissions officers say they don't even look at SAT scores except in certain special instances—such as when they don't have enough information about a particular applicant's high school. But this is almost never true. If your SAT scores are anywhere in your application folder (they might be on your high school transcript or in a letter from your principal in addition to being in ETS's score report), the people who read your application will look at them and be influenced by them, even if they have to peek. This is simply human nature.

THIS IS TRUE EVEN AT BOWDOIN AND BATES

Bowdoin and Bates, two fine liberal arts colleges in Maine, don't require their applicants to submit SAT scores. Does this mean they think the SAT is for the birds? Yes and no. Both colleges discovered that they didn't need the SAT to help them find good students. "We probably get a higher proportion of able students who have proven themselves to everyone but the College Board," said a spokesman for Bowdoin. Both colleges say the SAT is flawed. But admissions officers at both colleges are still affected by human nature. When they see low SAT scores in an applicant's folder, they can't help wondering, "Is this kid stupid?"

If you plan to apply to Bowdoin or Bates and if you did poorly on the SAT, for heaven's sake don't mention your low SAT scores in your application. If you have an interview with an admissions officer, don't say, "I'm sure glad you dropped your SAT requirement, because I got a 350 on Math 1." Bowdoin's admissions officers will probably *assume* that you didn't do very well on the SAT if you don't submit your scores, but assuming is different from knowing. Don't give them a reason to doubt that you can make the grade.

The decisions at Bowdoin and Bates to drop the SAT were opposed by many faculty members who took the claims of the College Board at face value and believed the SAT was a good measure of "intelligence." Many of these faculty members still feel that way, and their opinions can put pressure, both directly and indirectly, on admissions committees. To talk about how poorly you did on the SAT is to risk making yourself seem undesirable as a candidate. Keep your scores to yourself.

WHAT ABOUT "NORMAL" COLLEGES?

If the admissions officers at Bowdoin and Bates think about SAT scores, you can imagine how much difference your scores can make at other selective colleges. If your SAT scores are anywhere in your application folder (and if you took the test, they probably will be), someone is going to see them and be affected by them one way or the other. "The first thing I look for is the scores," an admissions officer told us.

DON'T PANIC

Before you panic, keep in mind that the psychological importance of SAT scores in the minds of college admissions officers doesn't always work against you. In addition to being the most conspicuous item of information in your folder, your SAT scores are also the easiest to change in a short period of time. There's nothing you can do about the grades you have already earned. There's nothing you can do about all the extracurricular activities you never took part in. There's nothing you can do about the time you wrecked the principal's car. But you *can* raise your SAT scores in the space of just a few months.

WHOM DO YOU BELIEVE?

ETS and the College Board have claimed for decades that SAT scores can't be improved significantly through coaching. They even have statistics to support their claim. But the Princeton Review has proved conclusively that ETS and the College Board are wrong. You can learn to do better on the SAT in precisely the same way you would learn to do better in your chemistry class: by learning the material on which you are going to be tested.

If your teacher gave you a D on a chemistry test, what would you do? You'd probably say to yourself, "I should have worked harder," or "I could have done better if I'd studied more." This is exactly the attitude you should have about the SAT. If you were disappointed by your score on the PSAT, you shouldn't think "I'm stupid"; you should think, "I need to get better at taking this test."

HOW CAN I GET BETTER AT TAKING THE SAT?

Naturally, we'd be thrilled if you signed up to take our course at one of the Princeton Review sites around the country. We'd also be overjoyed if you bought our best-selling book, *Cracking the SAT and PSAT* or visited our website, where you can take a free practice test.

Our coaching course is very different from others. Our classes are small (eight to twelve students) and they're based on shared ability. Each student receives personal attention. When a student doesn't understand something in class, we work with him or her in even smaller groups, and then in one-on-one tutoring. Our teachers are sharp and enthusiastic. They did well on their SATs and graduated recently from top colleges. You'd like them.

Finally, we do our homework. Every year, we spend hundreds of thousands of dollars writing, improving, and updating our course materials. This is especially important when the format or content of the exam changes. When the SAT changes in March 2005, our materials will reflect the changes and our diagnostic exams will represent the new format.

ARE OTHER COACHING COURSES ANY GOOD?

That depends. There are some good coaches out there, but there are also lots and lots of bad ones. Well-meaning but misinformed guidance counselors spread an enormous quantity of misinformation about the SAT every year.

A good way to tell whether SAT coaches know what they're talking about is to ask them whether you should guess on the test. If the coach says "no," you can be sure that he doesn't know what he's talking about. Intelligent guessing is one of the keys to doing better on the SAT. It's a topic on which we focus a lot of attention in our school and in our book.

Some coaches will tell you that you should only guess on the SAT if you can eliminate three answer choices. This is also wrong. If you are able to eliminate just one choice on an SAT question, you will be likely to improve your score by guessing randomly among the remaining choices. Most students don't guess enough on the SAT, and the ones who do guess usually don't do it effectively.

Some students receive so much conflicting information about the SAT that they don't know what to think. One of our best students (her scores went up more than 250 points after taking our course) told us about the experience she had had before she came to us. "Every one of my teachers told us something different," she said. "My math teacher said we should never guess, because we'd lose points if we did, and that we should never go back and change an answer. My English teacher said we could guess, but only if we had narrowed it down to two possible choices. She also said we should double-check our work. My guidance counselor said we should always pick choice C when we guessed. It was insane."

Getting a lot of conflicting advice like this can be doubly damaging: It can confuse you as you prepare for the test, and it can make you freeze up when you're actually taking it. If you sit there in the test center trying to decide whether or not to guess, while the clock ticks and your pencil trembles in your hand, you'll lose points unnecessarily.

WHAT DO COLLEGES THINK ABOUT COACHING?

College admissions officers have peculiar feelings about coaching. Most admissions officers nowadays do believe that coaching can improve SAT scores. At the same time, though, they believe that the SAT is a good measure of preparation for college. As a result, they tend to look down on students whose scores they suspect of having been raised through coaching. This means that if you take a coaching course, you shouldn't say so in your interview. If one of your college applications asks you how you spent your summer vacation, for goodness sake don't say you spent it with Stanley Kaplan.

Coaching puts students in a double bind. You'd probably be crazy not to prepare for the test. But if you prepare for the test, you'll probably have to pretend you didn't. If people were rational about the SAT, this problem wouldn't exist. But people are most definitely not rational about the SAT, and they give no indication that they are going to *become* rational any time in the foreseeable future.

Many college admissions officers actually deduct points from the SAT scores of students they assume have been coached for the test. If you attend a private school in New York City, Ivy League admissions officers will probably take it for granted that you took a coaching course. You should keep this in mind as you try to decide whether to take one.

WHEN DO I START?

Admissions officers often assume you've been coached if your scores rise by more than a hundred points or so between the first and second times you take the test, or between the time you take the PSAT and the time you take the SAT. What this means is that the earlier you begin preparing for the SAT, the better off you're going to be. You'll be better off if you get your scores up before any numbers go into your permanent record.

Some people advise taking a coaching course during ninth grade. For the most part, we don't agree. That's because the SAT involves some math concepts you're going to learn in the tenth grade and, more importantly, taking a coaching course that early only extends the college admissions frenzy (which is absurd enough as it is). The best time to earnestly prepare for the exam is during your junior year.

If standardized tests make you frantic, however, there are a couple of things you can do. First of all, familiarize yourself with the test. The best way to do this is to go online to www.princetonreview.com, or pick up a book of practice exams at your local bookstore. Get comfortable with the types of questions. The more you know about the test, the less intimidated you'll be.

If you feel you need more preparation—or if you have a shot at winning a National Merit Scholarship—consider the Princeton Review's PSAT preparation options during your sophomore year by going online or by contacting your local Princeton Review office (1-800-2-Review).

PREPARING FOR THE SAT

The following is a list of some of the things you need to do before you take the SAT:

1. Know the timetable.

The SAT is given seven times a year. If you go to a school with a strong college preparatory program, your guidance counselor will probably make certain that you don't miss any deadlines. If your school's guidance department is weak or understaffed, you need to take things into your own hands. Get a registration form from your guidance office in the first semester of your junior year. Along with the application you should be given a booklet called *Taking the SAT*, which contains a sample test. If you can't afford the registration fee, it will be waived. *Don't be afraid to ask for a fee waiver; too many students skip the test because they think they can't afford the fee. ETS and the College Board never spend more than a tiny fraction of the money they set aside each year for fees for students who can't pay, but you have to get one from you counselor. ETS won't send them to individuals.*

You can also get all the registration deadlines and information online at www.collegeboard.com. You can even register online.

Be sure you pay attention to deadlines. ETS and the College Board charge huge penalty fees for students who sign up late or take the test on a stand-by basis. When you receive your admission ticket to the test, be sure you look carefully at the test center to which you have been assigned. Don't assume that it will automatically be your own high school or your first choice. If you show up at the wrong location on Saturday morning, you could either miss the test entirely or have to pay a penalty fee.

2. Practice with the real SAT.

One of the best ways to learn about the SAT is to practice on real tests. The College Board publishes a collection of real tests called *10 Real SATs*. It's usually available in bookstores. You can also order it, and other collections of tests, from the College Board by going their website.

3. Don't pay attention to other SAT books.

Most SAT-preparation books (not including ours, of course) don't have much to do with the real test. Some were written years ago by "experts" who had little specific information to offer about real SATs, much less the most recent version. Sometimes following the advice in popular SAT guides can actually *hurt* your scores. One of the best-selling SAT books contains a strategy for solving SAT analogies that actually leads students to *incorrect* answers. Another includes drills for an item type that hasn't been used on the SAT in years.

4. Work on your vocabulary.

The verbal SAT is little more than a vocabulary test. Students with big vocabularies almost invariably earn high verbal SAT scores; students with small vocabularies almost invariably earn low ones. In March 2005, this will change to a degree because analogy questions will no longer be part of the exam, but a strong or weak vocabulary will still impact your performance on Sentence Completions.

To the extent that you need to improve your vocabulary, don't try to do it by memorizing the dictionary; you'll never get past the first page, and you won't learn any words that will help you on the test.

You also shouldn't try to prepare for the SAT by studying the word lists in most SAT-preparation books. These lists often contain hundreds of words that have never been tested, and never will be tested, on the SAT. Most of the words in the popular coaching books are just *too hard* to be used on real SATs. *Cracking the SAT and PSAT*, however, contains a word list called the Hit Parade, which consists of the actual words tested most frequently on the SAT. Our list contains just 250 words and helps you to focus on the words most frequently tested.

The Princeton Review also publishes books whose sole purpose is to provide you the vocabulary you need to do well in school, on standardized tests, and later, in the business world. Our popular *Word Smart* series allows you to review hundreds of words, complete with definitions, correct pronunciations, and sample sentences.

The best way to improve your vocabulary, however, is to read widely. This will not only help you on the SAT but also make you a smarter and more interesting person.

5. Take a math course.

Many schools permit their students to stop taking math courses in eleventh grade. Students who aren't currently taking math courses do worse on the math SAT than students who are. Even (or especially) if you struggle in math, you should consider signing up for more math at least for junior year. If you haven't taken Algebra II already, take it. If you have taken Algebra II, see if your school offers something like Pre-Calculus, College Math, or Advanced Algebra—some course for students who want to keep taking math but don't want to take the big plunge into calculus. If you just cannot stomach another math course, pick up The Princeton Review's award-winning *Math Smart*. It can teach you lots of what you need to know to do well on the SAT.

6. Don't go to bed at seven.

Some guidance counselors tell their students to get a lot of sleep the night before the SAT. This probably isn't a good idea. If you aren't used to sleeping twelve hours a night, doing so will just make you feel groggy.

A much better idea is to get up early each morning for the entire week before the test and do your homework before school. This will get your brain accustomed to functioning at that hour of the morning. You want to be sharp at test time.

ON THE DAY OF THE TEST AND BEYOND

1. Have proper identification.

You are supposed to take identification to your test center. ETS's definition of acceptable ID is "any official document bearing the candidate's name and photograph, or name and description (driver's license, school ID, or current passport)."

If you find yourself at the test center with *unacceptable* ID (one with name and signature only), you *should* be admitted anyway. According to the ETS rule book, you should be asked to fill out an identification verification form and then allowed to take the test. If you really do turn out to be yourself, your scores will count.

If you arrive without any identification at all, a literal-minded supervisor could turn you away. One of our students got around this problem in a creative way. When the proctor told her she couldn't take the test, she simply took out a blank sheet of paper, wrote out a brief description of herself, and signed it.

"That is *not* acceptable identification," the proctor said.

"I know," said the student. "But the rules say students with unacceptable ID can take the test and supply real ID later."

She was allowed to take the test. Another possibility is to ask permission to call home and have someone drop off your driver's license while you're taking the test. That way you can have everything cleared up before you leave.

2. Have enough No. 2 pencils

The only outside materials you are allowed to use on the test are No. 2 pencils (take four of them, all sharp), a calculator, and a watch (an absolute necessity). Proctors have occasionally confiscated stopwatches and travel clocks. Technically, you should be permitted to use these, but you can never tell with some proctors.

3. Take brain food.

Some proctors allow students to bring food into the test room; others don't. Take a soda and a candy bar with you and see what happens. If you open them quietly and don't flaunt them, they probably won't be confiscated. Save them until you're about halfway through the test. Remember that it takes about ten minutes for sugar to work its way to your tired brain. If the proctor yells at you, surrender them cheerfully and continue with the test.

Counting the time you spend sitting or standing around and the time your proctor spends reading instructions, you'll probably end up spending four or five hours at the test center. Eat a light breakfast before you go, but don't eat a big heavy meal that will make you feel sleepy for the first hour of the test.

4. Get comfortable.

You are going to be sitting in the same place for more than three hours, so make sure your desk isn't broken or unusually uncomfortable. If you are left-handed, ask for a left-handed desk. (The center may not have one, but it won't hurt to ask.) If the sun is in your eyes, ask to move. If the room is too dark, ask someone to turn on the lights. Don't hesitate to speak up. Some proctors just don't know what they're doing. If you know you're in the right, stick to your guns or ask to speak to the supervisor. (The proctor is the person in charge of your room; the supervisor is the person in charge of the entire test center.)

5. Make sure your booklet is complete.

Before you start the test, make sure your booklet is complete. You can quickly turn through all the pages without reading them. Booklets sometimes contain printing errors that make some pages impossible to read. Find out ahead of time and demand a new booklet if yours is defective. Don't, however, read questions or give the proctor the impression that you've started the test early. Also, check your answer sheet to make sure it isn't flawed.

6. You deserve a break.

You should get a five-minute break after the first hour of the test. Ask for it if your proctor doesn't give it to you. You should be allowed to go to the bathroom at this time. You should also be allowed to take another short break at your desk at the end of the second hour. The breaks are a very good idea. They let you clear your head. Insist on them.

7. Don't cancel your scores unless . . .

ETS allows you to cancel your SAT scores. You can cancel scores at the test center by asking your proctor for a "Cancellation Request Form." If you decide to cancel later on, you can do so by calling ETS or by going to their website. You must do this by the Wednesday following the test.

We recommend that you *not* cancel your scores unless you know you made so many errors, or left out so many questions, that your score will be unacceptably low. Don't cancel your scores because you have a bad feeling—students frequently have an exaggerated sense of how many mistakes they made, and it's possible you did much better than you realize.

8. Check your answer sheet.

Make sure you darken all your responses before the test is over. At the same time, erase any extraneous marks on the answer sheet. Seriously: A stray mark in the margin of your answer sheet can result in correct responses being marked wrong.

9. Check up on ETS.

Send away for ETS's Question and Answer Service (available only on certain test dates). It costs a little money, but it's worth it. You'll get back a copy of your answer sheet, a test booklet, and an answer key. Check your answers against the key and complain if you think you've been mis-scored. (Don't throw away the test booklet you receive from the Question and Answer Service. If you're planning to take the SAT again, save it for practice. If not, give it to your guidance counselor or school library.)

10. E-mail us.

If you have a problem with your test, e-mail us by going to our website (www.princetonreview.com). ETS is unbelievably slow about looking into complaints. They are not sympathetic to student concerns. We are.

IS ONCE ENOUGH?
IS THREE TIMES TOO MANY?

How many times should you take the SAT? That's a good question to which there is no simple answer. Most high school students should probably take it twice, once in the spring of their junior year and once in the fall of their senior year. If you go to a college preparatory high school, this is probably what you will be encouraged to do by your guidance counselor. Most students' scores go up the second time they take the test (although the higher your score is the first time, the less likely it will be to go up the second). You probably should *not* take the SAT more than three times. If you take the test repeatedly, admissions officers will think you are the testing equivalent of a grade-grubber. Applicants who appear pushy are always at a disadvantage, and applicants who take the SAT more than three times usually appear pushy.

However, there are exceptions to these general guidelines. These are spelled out below.

1. IF YOU ARE APPLYING TO A STATE UNIVERSITY

Many state colleges and universities use fairly strict formulas to determine who will be admitted and who will be rejected. There is no limitation on the number of times you can take the test. If your scores are close to meeting the formula for automatic acceptance at a school you want to attend, of course you should take the exam again, even if it is for the third or forth time.

2. IF YOU ARE A TERRIBLE TEST-TAKER

If you always do miserably on standardized tests (say, between 200 and 400 on each section of the SAT), and if you have gotten help from a coach but still have not improved, and if your grades are pretty good—you might consider taking the SAT only once. One set of terrible scores doesn't look as decisive as two. If you score 310 on Math the first time, scoring 320 the second time isn't going to make you a more attractive college candidate. If you have only one set of scores in your record, you will at least leave open the possibility that your performance was a fluke. (If you have a learning disability or perceptual problem that limits your performance on the test, check with your counselor or with the College Board. Special arrangements can be made for students who need them.)

3. IF YOU CAN WIN MONEY

Some colleges pay generous scholarships based on nothing more than a student's SAT scores. If you're close to the cutoff, go for it.

SAT II

ETS and the College Board also put out something called the SAT II Subject Tests. The SAT II is a battery of twenty-two tests that cover a variety of different subjects. And, as if the SAT weren't enough, most selective colleges require you to take one or more of these Subject Tests *in addition* to the SAT.

Admissions officers generally believe that the SAT measures what you are capable of doing. SAT II, on the other hand, is supposedly designed to measure what you have actually done. If you do better on the verbal portion of the SAT than on the SAT II Writing test, you will be said to be an "underachiever."

This is entirely unfounded. The SAT and SAT II are almost exactly the same kinds of tests, and they test almost exactly the same kinds of skills. As with the SAT, the best preparation for SAT II is a thorough grounding in test-taking skills and an understanding of how the test-makers think.

Here are a few other points to keep in mind about SAT II.

1. SHOP AROUND

Colleges that require SAT II tests usually suggest that you take three: Math IC or Math IIC, Writing, and one other test of your own choosing.

Math IIC isn't necessarily harder than Math IC. To be sure, the content on the IIC is more advanced, but which you should take depends on which math classes you've taken in school. If you're a junior in pre-calculus, you've studied the material tested in Math IIC more recently than the material tested in Math IC. You may thus find the more "advanced" test to be easier. Take sample tests to be sure.

If the choice of test is left up to you, shop around. Some of the tests are much easier than others. The Physics Subject Test, for example, is very hard, because most of the top science students in the country take physics; the Biology Subject Test is generally said to be the easiest; the Chemistry Subject Test is graded on a generous curve. If you do well in English class— and especially if you do well on multiple-choice reading comprehension questions—you will probably do well, or even extremely well, on the Literature test. (This test, which consists solely of reading comprehension questions, is not to be confused with the Writing test. The Literature test is usually overlooked, but many students say it's the easiest SAT II test there is.) Students who have taken foreign languages usually find the foreign language tests easy. Don't assume that any of the SAT II tests are hard. Check them out before you decide, and then take as many as you feel you can do well on.

Similarly, you should never take an SAT II that you won't do well on (unless it's required). To see why, consider these two students and their SAT II records

Joe Bloggs	*Joe Bloggs's Best Friend*
Math IC 600	Math I 600
Writing 540	Writing 540
Biology 610	Biology 610
French 500	
History 420	

Joe Bloggs did as well as his best friend on Math, Writing, and Biology. In addition, he took two more tests. So who has the better record? Joe's best friend does. Joe has given colleges two more reasons to reject him—two uninspiring scores. Three good scores is all anyone needs.

You aren't trying on hats when you take SAT II tests. You should take only those tests on which you are certain to do well.

Colleges will see your scores on every test you take, not just the three that may be required. For this reason, you should never take a few tests "just for practice," unless you are careful to cancel your scores. We knew of a student who, in order to get a feel for college entrance tests, took the tests in Hebrew and Physics, two subjects in which he was entirely ignorant. Instead of gaining experience, he blotted his record with two terrible scores.

2. DON'T ACT LIKE A NERD

If you're a dyed-in-the-wool pre-med, take something besides the math and science tests if possible. If you take Math IIC, Physics, and Chemistry, an admissions officer may decide you're a basket case. Some guides say it doesn't matter which tests you take, but it can. Doing well on a variety of SAT II tests is a relatively easy way to look like a broadly accomplished person.

3. PARLEZ-VOUS FRANÇAIS?

If you spent your first sixteen years living in Paris, by all means take the French SAT II. You have a skill few others have—show it.

4. THERE ARE TWO ENGLISH SUBJECT TESTS

ETS and the College Board offer two SAT II English Subject Tests. The Literature Test consists entirely of multiple-choice questions; the Writing Test consists of multiple-choice questions plus a short essay.

Which should you choose? That depends on your test-taking skills. We have had a great deal of success coaching students for both tests. Even students who can't write well can do extremely well on the essay version. Before making your decision, take sample versions of both tests. Keep in mind, also, that some colleges *require* the Writing Test.

5. HIGH ACHIEVEMENTS CAN REDEEM LOWER SATs

Many college admissions officers are going through a phase of preferring SAT II tests to SATs. Some colleges even give more weight to SAT II scores than they do to SATs.

THE ACT

The ACT is the college admissions test of the American College Testing Program. It is the SAT's one big competitor. Many people believe that the ACT is more achievement-oriented than the SAT is, but this claim is groundless. For all practical purposes, the ACT and the SAT are the same kind of test. (It is true, however, that some people consistently do better on one test than on the other.)

Many colleges will accept either your ACT scores or your SAT scores. If you do significantly better on one than on the other, you should submit scores to the colleges accordingly.

For the most part, the advice in this chapter regarding the SAT also applies to the ACT. In other words, you should take the ACT in your junior year, you should follow the same advice regarding the day of test and beyond, and you should prepare for the exam by taking academically challenging courses in high school, reading a lot, looking at sample exams, and taking a prep course if needed.

There are a few significant differences. First, the ACT provides score choice, meaning that you can choose which scores you want to send to the colleges if, in fact, you take the exam on multiple dates. Second, the ACT relies even less on vocabulary than the new SAT will. Third, there's no "guessing penalty" on the ACT, so you absolutely shouldn't leave any question blank under any circumstances. Forth, there are some significant content differences, though with the launch of the new SAT in March 2005, the content gap will close significantly.

To understand the differences and similarities between the two exams, it never hurts to go to our website and research both exams.

PSAT AND PLAN

The PSAT is a shorter version of the SAT. It was introduced years ago to give students practice with an ETS test before they were required to take the SAT. In 1973, ETS tied the PSAT to the National Merit Scholarship. Now, instead of being merely a "practice" SAT, the PSAT became a crucial test for many students. More and more of them started preparing for it. Responding to students' anxiety, some high schools started administering a practice PSAT at the start of the sophomore year. Further, as the distinction between the PSAT and SAT has blurred, an increasing number of high schools have begun including PSAT scores from both sophomore and junior years on students' transcripts, raising student anxieties even more. Instead of allaying fears, the PSAT has compounded them.

Since 1987, the American College Testing Program has been publishing a similar test called PLAN. Currently, PLAN is not attached to any scholarship program.

QUESTIONS AND ANSWERS

DON'T COLLEGES LOOK ONLY AT YOUR BEST SAT SCORES?

Different people will tell you different things about how colleges use SAT scores: They use only the best ones, they use only the worst ones, they use only the most recent ones, they use only the average of all of them, and so on. For the most part, none of this is true. Admissions officers usually end up seeing all of your SAT scores. If there's a low score in there, it will be noticed even if the school has a "policy" of using only the best score. Lower scores that stand out can also make colleges suspicious of your high scores.

Some students think they should take the SAT once for practice, just to get the feel of it, and then take it again later for real and have those scores reported. If you do this, keep in mind that unless you cancel those first "practice" scores before the Wednesday after you take the test, your first scores will appear on the score reports ETS sends out after you take the test a second time. Once your scores are in ETS's records, there's almost nothing you can do to get rid of them.

All of that said, many colleges are increasingly using the best scores of their applicants, even combining the student's best Math score and best Verbal score, even if those two scores occurred on different test dates. Researching the procedures at each school you are applying to will help you know how your scores will be used, but the best advice is to try to make this confusing mess a non-issue. By first taking unreported practice tests until you are fully prepared, you can then take the test for real when you are most likely to achieve your highest potential score, and be done with it.

IF MY SAT SCORES ARE LOW, SHOULD I EXPLAIN IN MY ESSAY?

Never, never, *never* try to explain away low SAT scores. Admissions officers have heard every excuse you could ever come up with, and they don't believe any of them. Talking about bad SAT scores only draws attention to them. (Incidentally, talking about good SAT scores reduces their value. If you did well on the SAT, don't brag about it. Everyone will notice without any help from you.)

SHOULD MY GUIDANCE COUNSELOR WRITE A LETTER EXPLAINING MY LOW SAT SCORES?

No, unless there is a real, certified, absolute, undeniable, incontrovertible excuse for how poorly you did. There are only about three such excuses, and they all involve physical illnesses or tragic accidents. *Don't* let your guidance counselor write a letter simply saying that you're smarter than your SAT scores indicate or that you freeze up on standardized tests.

SHOULD I FILL OUT THE STUDENT DESCRIPTIVE QUESTIONNAIRE (SDQ)?

When you sign up for the SAT, you'll be offered a chance to answer a lot of questions about your achievements, interests, goals, and family situation. We recommend that you *not* fill out this form.

There are several reasons. First, it's a bad idea in college admissions to answer questions you haven't been asked. If the college of your dreams wants to know how many of your brothers and sisters are in college, let it ask you. Everything you write down in the SDQ will be seen by the colleges to which you apply. If you say in it that you're planning to be a pre-med, and the colleges to which you've applied don't want any more pre-meds, you'll be out of luck. You also don't necessarily want to present yourself in the same way to every college to which you apply.

The SDQ is a big business for ETS and the College Board (they sell lists of names to military recruiters, among others) and a marketing tool for colleges. It doesn't help students. Don't waste your time; don't fill it out.

WHAT'S THE DIFFERENCE BETWEEN A 610 AND A 590?

More than twenty points. People are funny. They'll buy something for $99.99 that they would never buy for $100, even though there's only a penny's difference in the price. Admissions officers are the same way about SAT scores. The *real* difference between a 610 and a 590 is only one or two questions, but most admissions officers will view a 610 as a significantly better prospect than a 590 even though they view a 610 and a 630 as being about the same. If you come close to one of the hundred-point plateaus the first time you take the test, get some practice and take it again.

Do Ivy League colleges have minimum SAT requirements?

Most selective colleges say they don't have minimum SAT requirements, but in effect all of them do. The cutoff may be fairly informal, but it's still real. If you don't score above that cutoff (whatever it is) you won't have a chance.

Admissions officers at very selective colleges will often try to reassure applicants by pointing out, say, how many students they admit who have math scores below 550. But if you look carefully at who these students are, you usually discover that virtually all of them are minorities, athletes, children of alumni, or other special cases.

There's no way to know what the effective cutoff is for schools in which you may be interested. Unless you are a "special case" yourself, you should keep in mind that the *true* median score for Yale, Princeton, and other highly selective schools is probably higher than the one published in the big directories.

CHAPTER THREE:
GRADES AND
ACTIVITIES

If your SAT scores are terrible, you can probably improve them through coaching and hard work. If your grades are terrible, you're in a tight spot. Did we hear you say you're a first-semester senior?

You may be surprised to learn that much the same is true of extracurricular activities. If you've spent the last three years perfecting your PlayStation skills, you're not going to help your college admissions chances very much by running out and signing up for a lot of interesting after-school activities. Like grades, long-term commitments are what primarily interest colleges.

If you still have a year or two left before your applications are due, we can probably help you improve your chances of being admitted to the sort of college you want to attend, and maybe help you get a better and more interesting high school experience at the same time. And if you've been earning good grades and taking part in interesting activities all along, we can help you present your record on your application so that it places you in the best possible light.

WHY GRADES MATTER

College admissions officers are interested in many things, but they are primarily interested in making sure that the students they admit as freshmen won't all flunk out. All selective colleges want to fill their classes with students who are capable of doing the work. No college wants to traumatize its freshmen by throwing them into a situation they aren't equipped to handle.

Probably the best indication colleges have of how well you'll do in college is how well you've done in high school. Even the College Board and ETS admit that high school grades are better predictors of college success than SAT scores. As a result, colleges pay a lot of attention to the grades you've earned since ninth grade. The more successful you've been, the better your chances will be.

Each year, by the way, is more important than the last. Nothing looks better than steadily improving grades. Marks from junior and senior year are most important.

IS AN A ALWAYS AN A?

You are undoubtedly aware that different teachers at your school hand out grades in different ways. Some give A's to kids who do little more than show up every day. Others can't bring themselves to award anything higher than a B. Everybody knows stories like this. We heard about a teacher who had given extra credit to several students who helped him clean out his garage one weekend. This is very unfair, of course, unless you were one of the students who got the boost.

Much the same is true of different high schools. An A from your high school may be worth a lot more, in the mind of an admissions officer, than an A from a high school across town. It may also be worth less. It all depends on your school's grading policies and on admissions officers' familiarity with those policies.

When college admissions officers sit down to wade through each year's crop of applications, they decide how impressed they should be by individual transcripts. If they aren't familiar with your high school already, they need to know how to interpret your grades. They do this not only by trying to understand your school's grading system, but also by evaluating the caliber of courses you've been taking.

WHAT'S WRONG WITH THE COURSES I'VE BEEN TAKING?

Maybe nothing is wrong. But you shouldn't think that the A you earned in Film Comedy is going to shine as brightly as the A your best friend earned in Advanced Chemistry. All A's are not created equal. Anybody can inflate a grade point average by taking a lot of easy electives that don't require much thought or work. You (and your parents) may enjoy seeing the A's on your report cards, but don't expect college admissions officers to be as easily impressed by your transcript. The names of the courses you took are going to be printed right there next to the grades you earned. If the courses are dopey, the A's won't matter.

IS A B IN A HARD COURSE BETTER THAN AN A IN AN EASY COURSE?

This is a question that college admissions officers and guidance counselors hear all the time. They usually answer by saying that tough, academic courses are much better than frivolous ones and that grades in tough courses are given more weight than grades in easy ones. But you should keep in mind what Stanford reminds its applicants: "Be careful not to assume that the world is divided between students who take difficult courses and get B's and the students who take easy courses and get A's. Most of our applicants are able to take difficult courses and receive A's."

Of course, not everyone wants to go to Stanford, and not everyone can make straight A's. But the general principle always applies. If you can handle the work in honors, Advanced Placement, or other accelerated courses, you should probably be taking at least a few of them. (Many schools even add points to the grade point averages of students who take these harder courses.) If it is obvious from your transcript that you are taking a lighter load than you can handle, admissions officers at selective colleges are going to wonder about your motivation. They will be especially concerned if the difficulty of your course load drops off noticeably in eleventh grade.

On the other hand, a D in Advanced Placement history is not more impressive than a D in ceramics. It may even look worse. Don't get in over your head.

WHAT'S IN A NAME?

No matter what level you feel comfortable at, though, you should be aware of how your transcript will appear to admissions committees. Even if you can't handle accelerated work, you can at least stay away from the kinds of courses that set off alarms in the minds of admissions officers.

What kinds of courses are these? You probably know already. They're the electives you sign up for because they sound fun and easy: Children's Literature, Sailing, Hollywood Biographies, The Detective Novel, Darkroom Technique, History of Spaceflight, German Cooking, and independent study in almost anything. Courses like this began to abound in the late 1960s when students began to complain that traditional subjects weren't "relevant" to their lives. Many high school and college educators agreed at the time. The consensus has changed now, yet a lot of the old "electives" remain in high school curricula.

THE BIG TIP-OFF

One mistake many students make is to fill their schedules with easy electives as soon as they've fulfilled their schools' minimum academic requirements. That's what Joe Bloggs did. His high school requires two years of science, three years of math, one year of a foreign language, two years of history, and four years of English. By the time he'd finished tenth grade, he had satisfied all of these requirements except English and Math. He had never done well in math and science, so he didn't sign up for any science courses his junior year. Instead he took a pottery course and did an independent study on investing in the stock market. To satisfy his English requirement, he signed up for a course called Doonesbury, Peanuts, and Krazy Kat: The Literature of the Comics. He also took driver education, physical education, and photography.

Here's what Joe's transcript looked like by the end of his junior year.

Ninth Grade	*Tenth Grade*	*Eleventh Grade*
English 9	English 10	Literature
World History	U.S. History	Comics
Algebra I	Geometry	Independent
Earth Science	Biology	Study: Stock
Personal Hygiene	Spanish I	Market
Phys. Ed.	Phys. Ed.	Algebra II
		Pottery
		Driver Education
		Phys. Ed.

Never mind what Joe's grades were. The most important fact about Joe's transcript is the courses listed on it. There isn't an admissions officer in the country who wouldn't look at this transcript and think something like: "Joe decided to take a year off his junior year." Joe's college prospects will be even bleaker if he decides (as he probably will) to put together a similar schedule for his senior year, especially since his senior year doesn't even require a math class.

WHAT TO DO INSTEAD

The top college candidates in the country won't have transcripts that look anything like Joe's. They'll have taken courses like AP United States History, AP English, Calculus, Chemistry, Physics, French IV, and so on. If you can handle high-powered courses like that, you ought to be taking them. In addition to increasing your attractiveness to admissions officers, you'll be getting a better education.

But even if, like Joe Bloggs, you don't feel up to taking (or can't qualify for) a lot of accelerated courses, you can at least keep your transcript from looking like it belongs to someone whose mind is on vacation. Here are some specific tips, broken down by subject area.

English: Many high schools still permit students to satisfy English requirements with phony-sounding electives like Film Animation and Psychology of Advertising. If your school offers an English course simply called "English," that's probably what you should be taking. If you can't resist taking an elective, be sure the one you sign up for sounds serious. Shakespeare's Tragedies and Expository Writing are better than The Films of Woody Allen and Writing for Television. The very worst English electives are the ones that have nothing to do with

English, even if your school permits them to count towards an English requirement.

History: It is often somewhat easier to find history electives that sound both serious and interesting. Contemporary European History or the Russian Revolution wouldn't look bad on a transcript. Avoid courses on current events and ones that have clever names (for example, Riots and Revolutions). American history, European history and regional world history (History of the Middle East, History of Southeast Asia) are always good bets, and most schools offer several courses.

Math: Many students find math frightening and difficult. They eagerly look forward to the day when they'll finally have accumulated enough credits to be able to stop taking math courses altogether. They complain that algebra doesn't help them in their daily lives, and that it never will help them in their daily lives. Though they're probably right, they should keep in mind that math will be useful—not just for the SAT and transcript, but for majors like architecture, engineering, or any science.

If math baffles you, you don't need to sign up for Calculus, especially if you'd just earn bad grades in it anyway. Most schools do offer serious-sounding math courses—with names like Advanced Math or College Algebra—intended for students who don't want to knock themselves out in accelerated courses. You don't have to pretend that you want to be a mathematician when you grow up, but continuing with math in your transcript is a good way to keep from looking like a slacker.

Sciences: What we said about math courses also applies to science courses. And the closer you stick to the basic sciences (biology, chemistry, physics), the better off you'll be. Science courses in psychology, geology, astronomy, and similar subjects are less likely to seem impressive.

Foreign Language: One year of a foreign language doesn't look much better on a transcript than no years. Two years doesn't look much better than one. No one can learn to speak and read fluently in one or two years.

Taking three or more years of the *same* foreign language is a good way to add seriousness to your transcript. (Don't make the mistake of taking one year of French, one year of Spanish, and one year of German.) A long-term commitment to a language shows not only that you don't mind studying but also that you have the gumption to stick with something over a long period of time. If you took Latin last year, stick with it.

Languages offer another admissions bonus, too. When education critics talk about the "crisis in our schools," one thing they talk about is the decline in the teaching of foreign languages. Some schools no longer offer foreign languages at all. Taking languages makes you look like one of the old-fashioned, committed students that admissions officers dream about.

DON'T STOP WORKING

Virtually all colleges require your high school to update your transcript with a mid-year grade report in the middle of your senior year. If you slack off during the first semester of your senior year, you can ruin your chances of being admitted to a selective college. We know a student whose early acceptance was actually withdrawn because of his poor performance during the first semester of senior year. Colleges really do care about your first-semester senior grades. Be very careful. (Actually, you have to screw up pretty badly to have an acceptance withdrawn. But you might be surprised at how many students find ways to screw up pretty badly.)

What's more, some scholarships, especially at state universities, are offered solely on the basis of GPA or class rank, and these scholarships are often awarded well after the release of first-semester senior grades.

CLASS RANK

Many colleges say that class rank is more revealing than simple grade point average. (Most are interested in both.) Students who end up near the bottom of their high school classes tend to end up near the bottom of their college classes as well. The only way to move up in your class ranking is to earn better grades, or hope that those ahead of you decide to stop working so hard.

Some top college prep schools refuse to calculate exact class ranks because they believe a precise ranking would be misleading. At some competitive prep schools, the difference between, say, the tenth student and thirtieth student in a class of one hundred can be just a few tenths or even hundredths of a grade point. The tenth student might have a grade point average of 91.7 on a scale of 100, and the thirtieth might have an average of 90.9. The difference between those two students might be nothing more than a flunked geometry test in ninth grade.

If the grade point averages in your school are bunched up like this, be sure that your guidance counselor includes an explanatory note with your transcript (and those of other students from your school). Don't offer the explanation yourself, even if the application you're filling out provides a space in which you can "explain" unusual information. If an explanation is needed, it's better to have it come from someone other than you.

GRADING SYSTEMS

The same is true if your school uses a grading system that deviates in any way from one of the standard grading systems. If an 85 is counted as an A at your school, colleges should know. Admissions officers rely on high schools to help them understand peculiarities in the way they hand out grades. Good high schools routinely include explanations of their grading systems with the transcripts of their students. (They also include other information about the way they operate.) If your school doesn't do this, it should, especially if your school has never or has only rarely sent students to the colleges to which you are applying. Admissions officers never feel they have too much information about the high schools from which they receive applicants.

Making sure colleges have enough information is especially important if your school is in any way unusual. One high school we know about requires all its students to take a course called Interpersonal Relationships. A course with a name like that might sound like a hokey elective on your transcript; the colleges you apply to should know that you had no choice about taking it.

It would usually be ill-advised for *you* to explain your school's grading system. Just check with your guidance counselor to be sure your school is providing enough information to enable colleges to give you a fair shake.

PASS/FAIL

Never take a course pass/fail. Admissions officers don't know what to make of a "pass" on your transcript. They may count it as a C or even a D in calculating your grade point average. They will certainly decide that you were coasting when you took that course. At the very least you should never take a solid academic course pass/fail. (You may have no choice about taking some courses, like driver education and typing, pass/fail; that's not what we're talking about.)

If you go to a high school that doesn't give grades or that gives written evaluations instead of grades, your SAT and Achievement scores are going to be given much, much more weight than they might be otherwise, and it would be to your advantage to prepare very carefully for the tests. Unfortunately, high schools that don't offer a mainstream education usually don't prepare students very well for tests like the SAT. Their curricula don't emphasize the cut-and-dried basics (like arithmetic and vocabulary) that are the heart of the SAT. Even more important, these schools are seldom tuned to the same unimaginative wavelength that emanates from ETS. At The Princeton

Review, we regularly teach a large number of students from a high school that one of our teachers refers to as a "hippie school." The students are quite bright, but they read too much into straightforward SAT questions and their scores suffer as a result. Teaching these students is hard, because we have to show them a whole new way of thinking—the way of thinking that flourishes at ETS. Then, after their three-hour battle with ETS on a Saturday morning, they can go back to being their old creative selves.

EXTRACURRICULAR ACTIVITIES

Colleges want students who are capable of doing college-level work. They also want students who are interesting. To a large extent, a college's opinion of how interesting you are will be determined by what you do when you're not in class. Your extracurricular activities can play a big part in distinguishing you from other applicants and determining your chances for admission.

The following are some guidelines regarding extracurricular activities:

1. Quantity is less important than quality and commitment.

Some students think that the way to impress an admissions officer is to sign up for every activity their school offers. This is not a good idea. Colleges are not impressed by students with one of everything on their applications—one year of glee club, one year of yearbook, or one year of soccer. You're much better off if you're deeply involved in just a few activities that you remain committed to year after year. Colleges want to see students who rise to leadership positions in interesting activities. They want to see a student who is sports reporter for the school newspaper as a freshman, assistant sports editor as a sophomore, managing editor as a junior, and editor in chief as a senior. The way to impress an admissions officer is to demonstrate that you can stick with something long enough to become a big deal. You want to demonstrate that you can be a leader.

This doesn't mean you can't become involved in lots of different activities, especially if you have a genuine interest in lots of different things. Well-rounded applicants are very attractive to admissions committees. Yet, to the extent that it's possible, you should try to focus your energies enough to enable you to stand out. Just as it is better to take three years of French than to take one year each of French, Spanish, and German, it is better to spend three years rising to a position of importance on the student council than it is to join every organization that comes to mind.

2. You don't have to mention all your activities on your application.

Don't try to squeeze in every single activity you've ever been involved in—from a bake sale in ninth grade to the cleanup committee for the junior prom—in the belief that this will impress an admissions officer. Don't pad your list of activities. Concentrate on the ones that were most important to you (and that you were most important in) and don't be afraid to leave out ones that were trivial.

To give you an idea of what we mean, take a look at the following two lists. The first list is an actual listing of activities by one of our students. The second list is *our* version of the same list. Notice that our version is shorter and in a different order.

First Version

AFS 10

6th Grade Teacher's Assistant 11

Student Senate 10, 11, 12; Secretary 11, President 12

Yearbook 9

Wrestling 9

Delta Club 10, 11, 12

Anrig Award 12

Newspaper 10, 11, 12; Associate Editor 12

Tennis 9, 10, 11, 12; Co-captain 12

Lettermen's Club 10, 11, 12

Revised Version

Student Senate 10, 11, 12; Secretary 11, President 12

Newspaper 10, 11, 12; Associate Editor 12

Delta Club (community service) 10, 11, 12; Hospital Fund Organizer 12

Tennis 9, 10, 11, 12; Co-captain 12, State Runner-up Doubles 12

Anrig Award (scholarship and school spirit) 12

As you can see from either list, this kid is no slouch. But notice how much more impact the revised list has. In the first list, the student simply listed his activities as he remembered them, with no logic to the order. In our revision, we pruned out the skimpier-sounding activities and strengthened the important ones. AFS, sixth grade teacher's assistant, yearbook, and wrestling got too little of the student's time and attention to deserve mentioning. Including such halfhearted activities in a list actually weakens it, because they distract attention from the truly important and impressive activities. They also raise questions ("Why did he stop teaching?"). The Delta Club and the Anrig Award both needed explaining: An admissions officer isn't going to know what they are. We added an important accomplishment to the tennis listing. We left off the Lettermen's Club simply because it seemed unnecessary after the tennis listing (obviously this kid earned his varsity letter). If he had been an officer of the Lettermen's Club, we would have left it in and mentioned that, but he wasn't.

Of course, ours isn't the only way. How you write your list will depend on, among other things, how much space you are given in which to write it. And there aren't many students who have this sort of material to work with. But the general principle always applies. Trying to fatten up a list of activities often just makes it look thin.

3. All extracurricular activities are not equally impressive.

As we implied in the previous section, some activities are more important than others. Here are some of the more impressive activities.

- Student newspaper, especially in leadership positions.

- Student government, especially if you hold an executive office.

- Choir or orchestra, especially if you are a soloist or an officer.

- Varsity sports, particularly if you are a captain or an all-star of some kind.

- Leadership positions with substantial time commitment in organizations or community service activities.

- Activities with a special significance at your school or in your community. If the Harvest Queen is the most important person at your school—more important than the president of the student council—and you are the Harvest Queen, don't forget to mention it and explain.

- Anything unusual that took a lot of time and effort, such as being mayor of your town or a volunteer firefighter.

- Eagle Scouts.

- All-state anything.

- Math club (if you're female).

Here are some activities you probably shouldn't mention in your application. (We're not saying don't participate in them; just don't talk about them in your application.)

- Science Fiction Club or any activity having to do with science fiction.

- Anything that would cause you to mention the words "Dungeons and Dragons" in your application.

- Game clubs, especially role-playing game clubs.

- Any radical political organization, especially any radical right-wing political organization.

- Any fundamentalist religious group.

- Any paramilitary or vigilante organization.

4. Remember why colleges are interested in extracurricular activities.

Colleges are most interested in students who do interesting things, stick with them, and rise to positions of leadership in them. Beyond this, they are most interested in activities that show you have the respect of your peers. You should be careful about putting too much emphasis on activities that don't bring you into contact with other people: reading, hiking, writing poetry. These are great activities and they're worth pursuing, but if they're important to you, you want to be sure you're also doing things that demonstrate your ability to be a leader and get along with groups of people.

Science fiction fantasy does not go over big on college applications. Keep it to yourself. If you don't, admissions officers will worry that you'll become so involved in your fantasy life that you'll get into trouble with your schoolwork.

Colleges also look for your involvement in activities that reinforce academic or other goals that you mention in your application. If you say in your application that writing is very important to you, you should emphasize activities that gave you opportunities to write.

5. Extracurricular activities can make up for less than stellar grades, but only somewhat.

Students who are deeply involved in extracurricular activities often find that their grades suffer as a result. Admissions officers understand this, but don't believe for a minute that your list of activities will completely make up for mediocre grades. If you want to attend one of the top colleges, remember that a lot of high school students are editors of their newspapers *and* straight-A students. Don't overextend yourself to the point where your grades truly suffer.

Simply put, activities add depth to a solid academic application; they don't redeem a poor one.

6. After-school jobs can be impressive, significant activities.

If you can't take part in extracurricular activities because you have to work after school, you won't necessarily be at a disadvantage. Work can be an impressive activity, and you should think about your job in the same way we've told you to think about your activities. You can use your job to convey what a good college candidate you are.

As with other extracurricular activities, the best after-school jobs are the ones you stick with for an extended period and ones in which you rise to positions of responsibility. Simply selling hamburgers at McDonald's is nothing special, but advancing to become a store manager is.

Unusual or creative jobs are better than ordinary after-school, minimum-wage drudgery. If you have the choice (and not everyone does), try to choose a job that makes you seem interesting. If you have to work so that your family can make ends meet, be sure the colleges you apply to know that. Helping to support a family is a serious, adult responsibility, and it demonstrates good character.

If the money you earn after school goes for luxuries like expensive clothes, you need to be a little careful about your after-school job. Some students become so wrapped up in earning money that they lose all interest in activities offered by or associated with their schools. A student who helps his family make ends meet looks like a good prospect to an admissions officer; a student who misses out on school government because he's working to meet payments on an SUV does not.

HOW I SPENT MY SUMMER VACATION

Most of what we've been saying about extracurricular activities and after-school jobs also applies to how you spend your summer vacations. If you have the luxury of choosing how you spend your summers, choose jobs and other activities that help make you the committed, interesting paragon that we've been describing.

QUESTIONS AND ANSWERS

SHOULD I GO TO SUMMER SCHOOL AT EXETER OR HARVARD?

Many prep schools and colleges earn money during the summer by conducting classes for high school students and others. Many students have the idea that enrolling in these summer sessions is a ticket to admission at very selective colleges. This is not the case.

First of all, summer sessions at these schools tend to be nowhere near as rigorous as their regular sessions. Surviving Harvard summer school won't make Harvard think you're capable of doing Harvard work.

Second, unless you have a pressing reason for attending one of these summer sessions, you would probably help your chances more by getting an interesting job. Don't sign up for summer school just because you think it will impress the admissions office at Princeton. It won't.

Still, there are certainly worse things you could do with your summer. And hanging out on a college campus between regular semesters can actually be a lot of fun. You're bound to learn something, and it beats mowing the lawn.

SHOULD I TAKE COURSES AT A LOCAL COLLEGE DURING THE SCHOOL YEAR?

If your high school really can't satisfy your academic needs (because it doesn't offer calculus or because you've taken all the science courses it offers), you shouldn't hesitate to turn to a local college. Some high schools even have formal arrangements with colleges in their areas. What you should never do, though, is go to a local college to take a course that your high school offers. If you simply look like you're trying to impress an admissions officer, an admissions officer probably won't be impressed.

If you do sign up for college courses, be careful that you don't accumulate too many college credits to be admitted as a freshman at the college you want to attend after high school. Some colleges and universities have restrictions on how many college credits their applicants can earn before matriculation. These figures vary from college to college, but in general it's best not to rack up more than one semester or two quarter's worth of hours if you want to be considered a freshman.

SHOULD I DROP AN EXTRACURRICULAR ACTIVITY I LOVE JUST BECAUSE YOU SAY IT ISN'T AS IMPRESSIVE TO ADMISSIONS OFFICERS AS SOME OTHER ACTIVITIES?

No. You shouldn't become so calculating that you end up doing a lot of things you don't like. It's senseless for you to sign up for some boring activity you hate, or to drop an activity that you like, simply because of its potential impact on your college applications. Make choices that are good for you, but also understand the impact that those choices will have on your college application. In most cases, this doesn't mean that you should add activities that you hate or drop activities that you enjoy. Instead, it simply means that you should know which of your activities to emphasize on your college applications. It also means that you should always try to demonstrate commitment and leadership in the activities that you enjoy participating in.

I GOT AN F IN MATH IN NINTH GRADE. AM I SCREWED?

No and yes. Admissions officers are pretty good about discounting isolated failures, as long as they happen early. If you blow off your entire ninth-grade year but then pull yourself together for the rest of high school, most admissions officers won't be unduly bothered, but it will certainly be noticed.

Keep in mind that even if an admissions officer looks past an F on your freshman transcript, you'll still be left with a grade point average and class rank that are lower than they might have been. When admissions officers flip through your file, they'll notice those numbers and very possibly forget all the ins and outs of your transcript.

I'M LISTED IN *WHO'S WHO AMONG AMERICAN HIGH SCHOOL STUDENTS.* SHOULD I MENTION THIS IN MY APPLICATION?

No. Being listed in the high school *Who's Who* is like being invited to join the National Geographic Society. It doesn't mean anything. Don't try to beef up your application with phony accomplishments. If admissions officers cared about *Who's Who Among American High School Students,* they'd order copies of it. They don't.

CHAPTER FOUR: YOUR APPLICATIONS

Most students hate filling out applications. They hate answering the questions, and they hate having to complete everything properly. This is good news for you, because it means that you can improve your chances substantially simply by paying more attention to these details than everybody else does.

In this chapter, we'll cover all the basics and alert you to some of the peculiarities you may encounter. Essay questions, faculty recommendations, and interviews are covered separately in Chapter Five.

ACCESSING APPLICATIONS

As we told you in Chapter One, you should write away for applications and other information, or go online to look at applications on college websites, no later than the summer before your senior year and no sooner than the spring of your junior year. Although we don't recommend applying to more than six schools, there's no reason not to look at applications from lots and lots of colleges. Sometimes you can tell from an application itself that a school just isn't the place for you.

If you want to complete applications the old-fashioned way, you can either download them from the college websites and then print them off, or you can write or e-mail the college and ask them to send you a paper copy. Alternatively, an increasing number of colleges will let you apply directly online. Better yet, you can go to www.princetonreview.com, set up a free account, and save colleges that you are considering in your online locker. Our website has links to hundreds of online college applications, so if you're applying to multiple schools (and you should), it's a good place to go to get everything done in one place.

ALTERNATIVES TO THE REGULAR ADMISSIONS PROCEDURE

Many colleges offer variations on the standard, single-deadline admission procedure. Here are the most important of these variations, with our comments.

1. ROLLING ADMISSIONS

Some schools, primarily big state universities, don't admit their freshmen all at once: They admit them as they go along. If you apply in October, your application is considered in October. If you apply in November, your application is considered in November. Admissions officers keep accepting (and rejecting) students until they have filled the freshman class.

If you are applying to a school that uses rolling admission, it is obviously in your best interest to apply as early as possible. The longer you wait, the more likely you are to be rejected simply for lack of space.

2. EARLY DECISION

Some colleges conduct a special admission period before their regular admission period. If you know absolutely that you want to attend a certain college, you may be able to apply early and be notified of your acceptance, deferral, or rejection before your classmates have even begun to fill out their applications. Deadlines for early-decision programs usually fall in November; notifications are usually made in December.

Colleges expect something in return for giving you the chance to do this: a binding commitment from you to attend their college if you are accepted. Some colleges don't even permit early-decision candidates to apply to other schools until after the notification date. This means that you shouldn't apply Early Decision unless you are sure you want to attend that school.

If you have, in fact, determined your top choice by October, Early Decision is a great option, especially if you have strong credentials. Many top colleges admit an increasingly large chunk of their freshmen class through Early Decision. They like to lock in the strong candidates early, but this means that there are fewer spots left to be filled during the regular admissions cycle.

If your Early Decision application is rejected, you might be deferred to the regular admissions process, at which time the admissions committee will review your file again. This time, the pool of applicants that you are competing against will probably not be as strong, but again, there will be a whole lot more applicants in the regular admissions pool. Fewer open slots will be available because Early Decision acceptees will have filled a big chunk of them.

Keep in mind that if you are rejected Early Decision, it's hard to then be accepted during the regular decision process, since your application won't be read entirely in a fresh light. After all, admissions committee members at that college have already rejected your application once. Because of this, some counselors advise that if you have good but not excellent credentials, you should apply regular decision. Your application will compare favorably to the rest of the regular decision pool, but a bit tarnished if it had already been viewed as mediocre when compared to the Early Decision pool.

It's hard to predict what will happen in your particular case, but everyone agrees that there are a few things you should always remember if you decide to apply Early Decision.

- Early Decision is a good way to let a college know that it is your top choice. Colleges love to be loved. They'll look favorably on you for having the good taste to love them.

- Students who are accepted Early Decision often end up blowing off their second semester senior grades. Don't let your grades fall too dramatically. It's not unheard of that a college will rescind its offer if you really blow it. What's more, in some cases your scholarship package may be dependent on your high school grades.

- An Early Decision acceptance can save you lots of time and money. After all, you won't have to fill out lots of other applications. You can focus your time in the winter and spring on completing the financial aid and housing forms, and generally planning your future, without having to wonder for months where you'll be living in the fall.

- Since Early Decision is binding, an acceptance closes the door on your ability to compare financial aid offers from other schools.

3. EARLY ACTION

Some schools offer a variation of Early Decision known as Early Action. The best thing about Early Action is that it is non-binding. If you get accepted, you can still apply to other schools. If you don't get accepted, however, it's difficult to get accepted to the same university during the regular admissions cycle. Like Early Decision, Early Action candidates are generally highly qualified. Strong but not excellent applicants might be better advised to apply during the regular decision cycle to increase the chances of acceptance. On the other hand, if you're not set on attending a particular college, and if you are willing to fill out regular decision applications for several other colleges that are good fits for you, it might be worth it to apply Early Action to a college. If you're accepted, you can still apply to those other colleges if you change your mind; if you're rejected then other great alternatives are still available to you.

EARLY IS BETTER THAN LATE

No matter how you apply, it's always better to get your application in early than to wait till the last minute. Admissions officers generally *like* to admit students and feel sad about rejecting them. The earlier in the decision process your application is considered, the less likely it will be thrown irretrievably into the Reject Pile. Early in the process, admissions officers tend to be more forgiving of borderline applications than they are later on. It's toward the end of the admission period, when deadlines are approaching and when fewer slots remain, that admissions officers begin to get ruthless.

Remember that you will never get your application in early unless you start working on it promptly. Don't put it off. Many colleges will ask you for general information or ask you to fill out a preliminary application before you complete a full application. Do this right away.

GENERAL GUIDELINES FOR FILLING OUT APPLICATIONS

No two schools' application forms are exactly alike, although there are lots of similarities. Here are some tips and comments that will help you as you begin to complete them.

1. PAPER FORMS VERSES ONLINE APPLICATIONS

Completing your applications online just makes sense. It makes the whole process much more efficient. You don't have to figure out how to complete a paper form. You don't have to put the application in the mail. You can easily make adjustments before you send it. You can complete part of the application and return to it later without fear that, in the meantime, you'll misplace it or spill coffee on it. The benefits go on and on.

Still, if the college you're applying to requires all or part of the application to be submitted on paper, or if you're a tactile person and an online application gives you no satisfaction, you can complete the application the old-fashioned way. If you do, make sure you read the instructions on the application very carefully. Those instructions will outline precisely how you need to complete the application. They are often very specific, down to the size font you can use when you type your essays, or the color of ink you can use if you (gasp!) complete the application the old-old-fashioned way (which we don't recommend).

The cool thing is that if you mess up, you can download another copy from the college's website right away. Virtually all colleges deliberately make their forms very accessible. Just go to the college's website, click on admissions, and you'll easily be able to figure out what you need to click to get another copy.

If you have the option of applying online but you can't decide whether you want to use paper forms instead, we suggest you talk to four people: two people who filled out paper applications last year and two people who completed their applications online. We bet we know which ones were more frustrated.

2. A CONSISTENT STYLE

Newspapers and magazines all have style sheets or style books that allow their writers to remain consistent. They don't want to say "84th Street" today, "eighty-forth street" tomorrow, and "84 St." the next day. The style sheet spells out the rules. (We're not talking about writing style here, just consistency.)

You should have a consistent style, too. Consistency matters more than which particular style you choose. If you give your state's name as KS on the first line, don't give it as Kansas on the fifth.

3. SPELLING AND GRAMMAR

Misspellings in your application can make you look like a moron. Of course, presuming that you are either completing the application online or using a word processor to complete a paper form, you can use your spell check feature to find most of the mistakes.

But don't give your spell checker more credit than it deserves. It won't distinguish between "it's" and "its" since they're both correctly spelled words. Even some grammar checkers won't highlight all of those kinds of mistakes. What's more, your spell checker won't tell you how you should spell many proper nouns. Your spell checker might highlight an unknown word, but it's still up to you to make sure you've properly spelled that word. Don't skip past it too quickly in a mistaken presumption that you know how to spell something that in fact you don't. It's a good idea to double check anything that your spell checker highlights, just in case.

You couldn't do much worse than one girl we know about, who misspelled a college's name three or four times in her application. She was rejected. Imagine, for example, spelling Spelman, the correct spelling of the college in Atlanta, as Spellman. Or imagine spelling Denison as Dennison. Or Pittsburgh as Pittsburg. You get the idea.

Bottom line: students whose applications are filled with misspellings and poor grammar look like students who don't care.

4. PHOTOGRAPHS

Many colleges ask you to attach a photograph to your application. Usually the photograph is optional. What kind of picture should you attach? Should you attach one at all?

Admissions officers say that seeing photographs of applicants helps them think of applicants as people rather than as pieces of paper. This can work for you or against you. Under some circumstances you might be better off being considered a piece of paper.

Remember, the admissions committee members might be very reasonable, but they are human beings, and human beings react to pictures from a very deep level that is sometimes hard to consciously control. Applicants probably should not use photographs that make them look too glamorous, beautiful, or sexy. We all know some men out there who think that beautiful women are stupid; we all know some women who are jealous of beautiful women. Be sensible. Choose a picture that highlights your smile, not your body.

You should not attach a photograph in which you are poorly or messily dressed, or in which you look drugged or asleep. You should use one that makes you look bright, lively, and healthy, but again not glamorous or sexy. Don't use a funny picture or one that's too artsy. Don't use a photograph that shows you smoking a cigarette, holding a can of beer, or sitting in the front seat of your Porsche. You also shouldn't use a photograph that looks as though it is calculated to impress admissions officers such as a picture of you being given an award. (Although we do know a student from the Midwest who made a big hit with admissions officers at one school by using a picture of himself standing beside his prize-winning cow.) Because formal yearbook photos all look pretty much alike, you might consider not using yours. A clear, focused, head-and-shoulders color snapshot might be better.

5. INTENDED MAJOR

Some colleges and universities offer special programs such as nursing or engineering with separate admissions. If you're interested in one of these, you may have to declare your intentions on your application, or even fill out a special application. Read the fine print.

Many other colleges will ask you to state your probable major, if you know it. Be careful how you answer. Your response can affect your chances of being admitted. Here are some things to keep in mind:

- Be absolutely certain that your "intended" major is a major offered by the college. If you say you're going to be a journalism major, you'd better be certain the college *has* journalism majors. Remember that offering a course in a field is not the same thing as offering a major in it. If you declare your interest in a field that doesn't exist at that school, the admissions officers will think you are not serious.

- You should avoid mentioning the Joe Bloggs majors of pre-med, pre-law, and, to a lesser extent, business administration if you can help it. (Some schools have special pre-med and pre-law programs that you have to sign up for ahead of time, but most schools don't.) Frankly, admissions officers are sick to death of reading applications written by pre-professionals interested in earning money. The less you sound like them, the better off you'll be. We're not suggesting that you lie or change your career plans. We are suggesting that you declare "undecided" and thereby leave open the possibility that the admissions committee will see you as someone who possesses their ideal balance of career and educational goals. Uncertainty allows fantasies to remain a possibility.

- Don't claim that you want to be a math major (or an engineering major) if your math SAT scores are mediocre. Don't claim you want to be a biology major if your high school science grades were low. Colleges will hold it against you if your credentials don't back you up. They'll think you don't know what you're talking about.

- College administrators and professors have been complaining lately that students don't major in the humanities (literature, languages, art history, etc.) anymore. Saying you want to major in one of these, assuming you do, might be a good way to distinguish yourself from Joe Bloggs. Another good way to distinguish yourself is to major in, say, biology with no intention of going on to medical school. If you want to be a bio major but don't want to be a doctor, find a way to say so in your application. Again, don't lie and say you want to do something you don't. But if you want to do something they'll find attractive, by all means let them know.

6. INTENDED CAREER

Like Intended Major, "undecided" is the safest answer. Medicine and law are the worst. (This is sometimes just a trick question to find out if you're a pre-med.) Teaching is probably the best at the moment. But no one says seventeen- and eighteen-year-olds have to know what they're going to do with their lives. Some admissions officers *prefer* applicants who haven't made up their minds.

Almost as bad as saying you want to be a doctor or a lawyer is saying you want to "help people" or "work with people." These are Joe Bloggs answers, too, and admissions officers hear them constantly. There's nothing wrong with wanting to help people, but find something more specific to say.

7. ACTIVITIES, AWARDS, EMPLOYMENT

Unless you're specifically told to do something else, the order in which you list these should reflect some combination of their importance to you and their probable importance in the eyes of admissions officers. Concentrate on the areas in which you've made the longest commitment and achieved the most responsibility. Reread Chapter Three for more advice on how to present your activities. Don't feel you have to mention *everything*. If you list a lot of trivial activities, you'll appear as though you're trying to put one over on the admissions committee.

In listing jobs, you should make your jobs sound interesting if possible, but you shouldn't make it appear as though you've been reading one of those books on how to write a resume. If you spent the summer working as a housekeeper, say you were a housekeeper; don't say you were a "domestic engineer." If there was something truly unusual about what you did, be sure you get it in, but don't exaggerate. If you were editor in chief of your school newspaper, be sure to mention that, but don't add that you were "responsible for assigning, receiving, editing, typesetting, laying out, and pasting up articles on a wide variety of topics." That's what editors in chief are supposed to do. If you spell it all out, you'll sound like a huckster.

You should, however, go into specifics if the activity is unfamiliar or if you did something noteworthy that isn't mentioned anywhere else in your application. You should also mention specifics if the specifics aren't clearly implied in the name of the activity or your title. If you directed three student plays, don't just write down "Drama." Spell out what you did. But be straightforward about it.

8. TRAVEL

Many applications will ask you to list recent travel experiences. Admissions officers like students who've seen a bit of the country or the world. You want to be careful, though, not to sound like a little rich brat. Play down the glitzy side of your trips, if there was one. If you paid for all or part of your trip yourself, mention how you earned the money. Most interesting are trips that show creativity, initiative, and independence on your part, like the summer you spent leading an expedition across Nepal with the money you earned working for the Jet Propulsion Laboratory. Or the summer you road-tripped through the South with your sister to take your elderly neighbor to see her childhood home. Much less interesting is the clothes-buying jaunt to Paris you took with your stepmother.

9. ALUMNI RELATIVES

Most colleges will ask you if you have relatives who attended the same school. Children of alumni and other "legacies" have an admissions advantage everywhere. Don't leave anybody out. Pull the great aunt out of the attic.

10. OTHER COLLEGES

Some applications ask you list the other colleges to which you're applying. Admissions officers ask this because they want to get some idea of how serious you are about their school. If you list other schools that are less selective than their school, they'll know you probably aren't counting on being admitted to their school and that your realistic first choice is elsewhere. Everything else being equal, a school that perceives itself to be your first choice will give you a slight advantage over other similar applicants who they perceive to be less enthusiastic about attending their school.

How does a college know that it's your first choice? There are many ways, some direct and some indirect. An admissions officer may come right out and ask you in an interview. More important, though, are clues scattered throughout your application. If you are really enthusiastic about a school, your enthusiasm will show through. The depth of your familiarity with a college is also a good indication of the strength of your desire to go there. There's nothing wrong with letting each school know how much you value its particular strengths. Make them all feel wanted. You'll figure out what your first choice is when you have two or more acceptance letters.

Your list of other colleges (even the order in which you write it) will also give admissions officers a little peek into the way your mind works and how you evaluate your own abilities. If the schools you list are all less selective than your credentials suggest you could get into, admissions officers may decide you don't think much of your own academic abilities.

How you answer this question isn't that big a deal. But you can never tell what will stick in the mind of an admissions officer, and you should not be too hasty to fill in your answers. Don't lie. But if you're applying to a lot of dissimilar schools, your answer doesn't have to be exhaustive. No matter what, don't list more than four or five other schools. If you're applying very early in the application period, you can simply list one or two other schools and say you're undecided about others. Keep in mind that other forms in your file, such as your financial aid forms, may also list the colleges to which you're applying. The most important piece of advice we can give you also applies to every other question on every other application you fill out: Before you answer any question you should ask yourself, "What does my answer say about me?"

QUESTIONS AND ANSWERS

SHOULD I LIE?

Good question. Almost everybody asks it. Admissions officers say they can always tell when applicants are lying. That's a lie. But lying is a bad idea anyway. For one thing, it's hard to do. Liars have to have very good memories. They have to be able to tell the story the same way every time, which is a lot easier if the story is true.

It is possible and necessary to tell the truth without telling the *whole* truth. There is nothing wrong with being selective in what you talk about in your application. And there's nothing wrong with not answering questions that haven't been asked. If the application doesn't ask you if you were ever suspended, don't feel you have to confess that you were. If being editor of the literary magazine was a joke at your school, keep it to yourself.

SHOULD I TAKE ADVANTAGE OF THE COMMON APPLICATION?

Of course. Keep in mind that you'll have to fill out supplements for each college that uses it, but it's an efficient way to apply to multiple colleges, as long as they accept it. The websites of those colleges generally will link you directly to the common application website and then will also allow you to fill out their own supplements online.

Some people believe that using the Common Application will hurt their chances of acceptance at a particular school. They think that a college would prefer that students use their own applications, not some common one shared with others. That's just plain false. Colleges know that you're also applying to other colleges. It's no big secret. All the colleges that use the common application have voluntarily agreed to do so; they know that it makes life easier on applicants. It's also why they've enthusiastically moved forward with online applications. It just makes life easier for everyone.

Colleges want good, substantive applicants. They don't care if students use the Common Application or their own application. They just want as many good apps as possible so that they can be as choosy as possible.

WHAT IF THERE ISN'T ENOUGH ROOM TO FIT EVERYTHING IN?

Whether you're applying online or using paper application forms, you can get a very good idea of how much a college wants to hear about you by looking at how much room they've left for you to say it in. Generally speaking, they don't want you to add a lot of extra stuff that they're not asking about. Nor do they want you to give twenty examples when five would do. If they give you tiny spaces in which to list your activities, it's not because they think you weren't involved in very much. It's because they want you to be brief and to prioritize.

What if I win the Nobel Prize after I send in my application?

Write a letter letting the admissions office know. The letter will be placed in your folder.

Should I ever, ever, ever put a little smiley face anywhere on my application?

No. And keep the font plain and simple too. :)

CHAPTER FIVE:
ESSAYS,
RECOMMENDATIONS,
AND INTERVIEWS

For many students, writing application essays, securing good recommendations, and coming across well in interviews are the most unbearable parts of applying to college. They certainly require care and planning. But they don't have to make you depressed.

While your SAT scores and your grades will be the most conspicuous elements of your application folder, the real debate about whether to admit you or reject you may very well concern how you come across in your essays, recommendations, and interviews. If you handle them well, you can substantially increase your chances for admission.

WRITING ESSAYS: FUNDAMENTALS

Virtually all selective colleges will ask you to write at least one essay as part of your application. Admissions officers think of your essay as a little window into your personality. They also see it as evidence of how well you write, which is something they care about a great deal. Colleges are very worried that their students don't write as well as students did in the past. An applicant with strong writing skills has a very big edge.

An admissions officer explained it to us this way: "You just know that a kid who writes well is going to do well in college courses. When faculty members talk to us about admissions, writing comes up frequently. They say, 'When are you going to start admitting students who can write complete sentences?' Good writers make the professors happy, and happy professors make us happy. It's also usually true that a student who writes well enough to be noticed by an admissions officer will also have put together a solid record in high school. It's easy to admit a kid like that."

No guidebook can teach you how to write. Good writers don't become good writers by memorizing a few rules. But we can give you some guidelines that should help you avoid some major pitfalls.

1. Don't use six-dollar words.

One of the worst things young writers do is beef up their compositions by substituting long, difficult words for short, easy ones. Some students write a rough draft in their own words and then use a thesaurus to plug in big, impressive words.

Doing this is always obvious, and it is never impressive. A good writer can spot a "thesaurus-ized" composition a mile away. The reason is that the big, plugged-in words seldom mean exactly what the young writer thinks they do. There are few precise synonyms in English. Most of the big words in a thesaurus have meanings that differ from the meanings of the shorter words they replace.

2. Good writing is writing that is easily understood.

You want to get your point across, not bury it in words. Flowery writing is not good writing. Your prose should be clear and direct. You will be in trouble if an admissions officer has to struggle to figure out what you are trying to say.

3. Avoid adjectives and adverbs.

As you reread your essays, stop at every adjective or adverb and ask yourself if it is necessary. Too many adjectives and adverbs make writing seem flabby. Concentrate on nouns and verbs.

4. Avoid the word *however.*

However is a tricky word. Most people use it incorrectly or put it in places where it isn't needed. Few people know how to put punctuation around it. Everyone uses it too much.

5. Buy and read *The Elements of Style*, by William Strunk, Jr., and E. B. White.

This little book is a required investment for any writer. You'll use it again and again and again in college and beyond. If you do what it says, your writing will improve. Get a copy tomorrow and read it twice.

6. Avoid using exclamation points.

Except in dialogue when someone is screaming or otherwise carrying on, they're usually not needed!!!

7. Throw away your copy of *Bartlett's Familiar Quotations.*

One of the worst things a student essay can contain is a lot of sentences that begin, "As Shakespeare said . . ." or, "I am reminded of Tennyson's words . . ." Admissions officers will know you found these lines in a book of quotations. They won't think you pulled them out of your memory. Quotations make essays seem phony, not sophisticated.

Don't begin your essay with a little quotation, either—no matter how perfect it seems. And don't *ever* quote the lyrics of your favorite song.

8. Don't put quotation marks around words that aren't quotations.

Don't put quotation marks around a word just because it isn't quite the "right" word for what you want to say. If the word doesn't seem "right" without quotation marks around it, find one that does.

9. Don't say what you're going to say, say that you're going to say it, say it, say it again, and say that you've said it. Instead, simply say it.

Most student compositions have tedious introductions and conclusions that first announce and then repeat whatever is said between them. Most good writers don't write this way. Even if they did, you wouldn't have room to do it on your application. You want to make sure a reader understands what you're talking about, but you also want to be concise. You don't want to bore an already bored admissions officer with a boring introductory paragraph that does little more than repeat the question.

10. Have a good writer critique your essay. Have a good speller proofread it.

Admissions officers take it for granted that applicants get help with their essays. In fact, if you submit an essay that is filled with misspellings and grammatical errors, admissions officers will conclude not only that you don't know how to write but also that you aren't shrewd enough to get help. Ask your mom, dad, teacher, brother, sister, *someone* to read your essay and comment on it. (Does it sound phony? Is it clear? Do I get my point across? Is it boring? Are the jokes stupid?) Be especially careful about punctuation. Most high school students don't know where to put commas. Find someone who knows. You should also critique your own essay after letting it sit for at least a few days. The longer it sits, the more mistakes you'll be able to find.

Asking for help isn't cheating (although actually getting someone else to *write* your essay is).

11. Put a lid on it.

Unless they specifically tell you otherwise, admissions officers would prefer that you confine your responses to the spaces provided for them. Longer is not better. Don't add extra pages because you think length is impressive. It isn't. Your essay will be the zillionth essay exactly like it that most of its readers have read. Do them a favor and be brief.

If you do, indeed, succeed at writing a truly original essay, it is still far better to be brief and leave the reader craving more than to risk turning your original first page into a repetitive or tiring second.

WRITING ESSAYS: TOPICS, ATTITUDES, APPROACHES

Your newly honed writing skills won't do you much good if you don't have anything interesting to write about. Most of your essay topics will be assigned, but some will probably be left up to you. Even if they are assigned, you will have a great deal of leeway in terms of approach. Here are some guidelines that should help you zero in on a good topic or, if the topic is assigned, help you find an effective way to get your points across.

1. Don't repeat information from other parts of your application.

An application doesn't give you much room to make your case. Don't waste space by repeating yourself.

For example, an application may ask you on one page to list your extracurricular activities and on another to write a brief essay describing what your activities mean to you. Don't use the essay simply to repeat the list in expanded form. Admissions officers *hate* it.

Instead of repeating yourself, take advantage of the opportunity to expand on information you've already provided. Write about something interesting that you did or that happened to you in one of your activities. If your list of activities includes something really outstanding that won't be immediately obvious to an admissions officer, use this essay to make sure it comes across.

Consider completing, or at least outlining, all the other parts of your application before you write your essays. By "all parts," we even mean figuring out who is going to write your letters of recommendation and looking at your transcript to figure out what's included on it. There's good reason for this. You not only don't want to unnecessarily repeat yourself, you also want to make sure you don't leave something extremely important unsaid. By doing the rest of the application first, and by anticipating what your recommenders will write about you, you can then use the essays to help broaden out and balance the image that the other parts of the application portray.

2. In general, avoid generalities.

Admissions officers have to read an unbelievable number of essays, most of which are boring. You will find it harder to be boring if you write about particulars. If you are called upon to write about your extracurricular activities, don't write an essay about activities in general: "Extracurricular activities are important to me because they enable me to expand my horizons," etc. Instead, *narrow* your focus. Write about something particular that happened to you in a particular activity. It's the details that stick in a reader's mind, and it's the details that make your essay a unique one.

But make sure you pick interesting details. If you're writing about your trip to Europe, don't give your itinerary. Focus in on an interesting detail: a fascinating old man, the time you got lost in Florence, the day you helped a Parisian fix his car.

This rule even applies to questions that seem to *demand* general answers. For example, many colleges ask students to write a few paragraphs about why they want to attend that particular college. One popular answer has to do with the value of "obtaining a good liberal arts education," or something similar. This answer is about as interesting as a sleeping pill, and you probably don't mean it anyway. You may not be able to give a really truthful answer ("Because I want to ski all the time"), but you can at least try to give an interesting one. You might talk about a particular course you want to take, or about a specific gap in your knowledge that you want to fill. The less general and vague your answer is—and the more you actually mean it—the more likely it is to be interesting.

One good way to avoid generalities is to write about people. Instead of writing about "a good liberal arts education," write about a person you admire who went to the same college. Instead of writing about how well your high school education prepared you for college, write about a teacher who made a big impression on you. The more specific you are, the more readable your essay will be.

Sometimes an application will try to nudge you in this direction by giving you a fairly specific question to answer ("Describe a teacher who meant a lot to you"). Don't defeat the purpose of this kind of question by hurrying as quickly as possible back into generalities. That is, don't write about a teacher who changed your life by showing you "the value of a good liberal arts education."

3. Be humorous if you can, but be careful.

One good joke can get you into Yale. No kidding. A student who can make an admissions officer laugh never gets lost in the shuffle. A witty observation is read aloud, everyone smiles, and no one can bear to throw you into the reject pile.

But beware. Most people think they're funny, but only a few really are. Most attempts at humor in college applications are counterproductive. Humor can help you, but you must use it carefully and sparingly.

In general, you will be better off if you strive to make your reader smile, not laugh. The closer you stick to your own life and your own experiences, the more successful you will be. Most of us are more successful at recounting humorous incidents from our lives than at making up jokes from scratch.

Most writers ruin jokes by beating readers over the head with them. Don't write, "A funny thing that happened to me the other day was . . ." or "I really had to laugh when . . ." If your story is really funny, you don't need to label it. And don't do the equivalent of nudging your reader with your elbow. The most successful joke is often the one told with a straight face.

4. Maintain the proper tone.

Your essay should be informal without being sloppy, witty without being childish, memorable without being outrageous. If read aloud, your essay should sound like good conversation. You want to warm your reader, not overwhelm him or her. You want to be casual without being chatty or cutesy.

5. Don't write about what Joe Bloggs writes about.

An article about college admissions in *The Kansas City Star* years ago described the essay-reading experience of Parke Muth, assistant dean of admissions at the University of Virginia: "This last academic year, Mr. Muth says, his university received 16,000 applications for 2,600 places, and he read 3,000 essays on participation in a summer program for gifted students and 3,000 on the students' travels around Europe with the theme 'It's a small world, after all.'"

What was true at Virginia years ago is still true today at every college. Students are still writing about the same things.

Here are some other topics you should probably avoid. Some of them are simply bad topics that are inappropriate for college applications. Others are extremely popular topics that make admissions officers' eyes glaze over. For one reason or another, don't write about the following:

- Your relationship with your girlfriend or your boyfriend. Important to you, but a little creepy to an admissions officer.

- Your religious beliefs. Deeply religious students make admissions officers nervous—*unless you're applying to a college with a strong religious orientation*, in which case an essay about your religious views would probably be in order.

- Your conservative political views.

- Any other political views. Have you ever had a political discussion with someone who didn't agree with you? Did you end up shouting at each other? People have a tendency to become upset very quickly with people whose political beliefs are different from their own. Avoid politics altogether and you won't run the risk of offending a reader. If you do write about a political experience—say, the summer you spent working on a congressman's reelection campaign— avoid ideology as much as possible and write about the nuts and bolts of running the campaign.

- The evils of drugs. Drugs are indeed evil, but student essays on this subject tend to sound goody-goodyish and contrived.

- The pleasures of drugs. For obvious reasons.

- Sex.

- The first time you got drunk, or any other time you got drunk.

- A classmate who was killed in a car accident. This is a standard topic, seldom handled well. Death is very hard to write about. Student essays about the death of a friend or family member are sometimes extraordinarily moving; more often, though, they sound either contrived or overly emotional. If you decide to write about a topic like this, be sure you're up to it.

- How much you love yourself. Don't write an essay that makes it sound as though you spend a lot of time sitting around thinking about yourself. All adolescents spend a lot of time thinking about themselves. Adults are tired of hearing about it.

- The importance of a college education. There just aren't that many observations you could make that an admissions officer wouldn't have heard a million times before. Joe Bloggs is irresistibly attracted to this topic, because he thinks it will make him seem serious. Instead, it usually makes him seem vacuous.

- Your personal philosophy, particularly if it involves any form of selfishness. Many, many essays are some variation on this theme. Generally speaking, *nobody's* personal philosophy is very interesting to anyone else.

- Your SAT scores. Never, never, never mention your SAT scores, no matter how good or how bad. In fact, never mention them again to anyone.

- How much you like to party, screw around, etc.

- Any topic that doesn't appeal to you but that you think will appeal to an admissions officer, such as how you have recently discovered the importance of studying hard. Essays like this make the Phoniness Alarms go off.

- Anything that will make a reader blush or feel embarrassed.

- Anything that will incidentally reveal you to be a poor college prospect—such as an essay on how much you hate to study.

- Big ideas, such as your plan for how to make the world live together in peace. These almost always flop. Stick to details and particulars.

- Trendy topics, such as globalization, the threat of terrorism, or anything involving current events. You probably won't come up with anything new to say. These essays, no matter what the intentions of the writer, tend to be predictable and boring.

- Anything that makes it sound as though the only reason you want to go to college is so you can make a whole lot of money when you get out. Admissions officers don't make much money, and they're sick of greedy teenagers.

- Solitary pursuits. In general, activities that involve interacting with other people make better topics than activities you do alone. You don't want to make admissions officers worry that you won't get along with your classmates. This is really only a problem if virtually every activity you mention in your application is solitary.

- How much therapy has changed your life. You don't want admissions officers to worry that there is a danger of your going crazy while in school.

- How glad you are to be a National Merit semifinalist or how pleased you were to be named valedictorian of your class. This is like writing about your SAT scores.

- "The Best Game of My Life" or any other athletic incidents written in glib style.

- Any topic specifically mentioned as a great essay topic in a popular how-to-get-into-college book. Joe Bloggs reads those books, too.

6. Write about something you really care about.

Even genuinely bad writers can turn out a readable essay if the topic means something to them. The motorcycle you built from scratch, the time you helped deliver a baby in a snowstorm, the day you taught your little brother to tie his shoes. The good topic is the one you *want* to write about, not the one you think you *ought* to write about—while always keeping in mind who your audience is.

The way to approach finding a topic is first to ask yourself what you want to write and then to ask yourself whether an admissions officer will want to read it.

7. Remember what the point of an application essay is.

With your essay you want to prove two things: that you are a decent writer and that you are an interesting, mature person. By contrast, Joe Bloggs thinks that the point of his essay is to prove to the admissions committee that he is serious about education. Admissions officers hear this constantly, and it bores them. "My summer in France taught me the value of a solid background in a foreign language . . ."; "The summer I spent at Andover summer school showed me the value of good study skills . . ."; "I never realized how important a good education was until. . . ." Nobody *really* thinks like this. It almost always sounds contrived in an essay.

Instead of trying to think of things you've done that will make you seem more serious, try to think of things that have made you more interesting.

8. Every story doesn't need a moral.

Many students feel they have to make a direct connection between whatever they write about and their suitability for college. Many essays convey the impression that their authors have never done anything that didn't groom them in some way for higher education. This, too, sounds contrived. If you write a good essay, you won't need to tell admissions officers why you wrote it.

9. Don't apologize; don't explain.

Don't use an essay to explain bad grades, low SAT scores, drug arrests, suspensions, or any other black marks in your record, unless the question on the application specifically asks you to do so. Explanations usually just make these sound worse. They certainly draw attention to your weaknesses.

If there really is something about your grades that should be explained, your guidance counselor should do it. But don't ask your guidance counselor to write a letter simply explaining that you are smarter than your SAT scores. It may be true, but admissions officers have heard it a million times.

Some applications will allow you to explain peculiarities in your record that you think need explaining. You may do so if you feel you must, but tread carefully here. Explaining a difficulty often does little more than draw attention to it, which makes it seem worse.

If an application asks you right out, as some do, whether you have ever been suspended and why, you'll have to answer truthfully. But unless you have a very, very good reason for doing so, you shouldn't answer this question unless it is asked.

10. Submit extra materials if they're called for.

Some colleges permit you to submit extra materials—poems, musical compositions or tapes, short stories, artwork, and so on. Some colleges don't want you to do this, and say so in their applications. Check on this.

Anything extra that you submit should genuinely enhance your application. Be realistic about your abilities. Submitting half a dozen unexceptional poems will make the poetry award you won seem less impressive. The same might be true of stories you wrote for a local newspaper. Before you let admissions officers see exactly what you did, be certain it doesn't sound better in the abstract.

Don't try to be too cute with extra submissions. Applicants sometimes endear themselves to admissions committees by sending homemade cookies or other clever creations. But be very careful. Gimmicky extras like this usually backfire.

Whatever you do, make certain your submissions are neat and well presented.

TYPICAL QUESTIONS, TYPICAL ANSWERS

Here's a selection of common types of essay questions, followed by some Joe Bloggs responses to them and recommendations for avoiding the Joe Bloggs mentality.

1. Write about someone you admire.

This question has many forms. Denison University's is "Indicate a person who has had a significant influence on you, and describe that influence." Joe Bloggs tends to write without much conviction about people like the president of the United States, his father (Joseph Bloggs, Sr.), Mother Teresa, or Martin Luther King, Jr. These may all be highly admirable, heroic people, but they seldom inspire interesting essays. The best responses are ones that are both meaningful to the writer and somewhat surprising to the reader. You don't want to *stun* the reader (by writing about Hitler, for example—never a good idea), but you do want to give him or her something unusual to think about.

2. Write about something you have read.

A number of colleges will ask you some version of this question. Many applicants are attracted to it because it seems so easy—all you have to do is write a book report. But that's the danger: Too many responses to this sort of question sound like book reports, and nobody likes to read book reports. The advice we gave you about the "someone you admire" question applies to this one as well: Don't write about an obvious book. Your choice should make you seem interesting (though not eccentric).

Most important, if you are asked to write about a book, be certain you write about a book: Don't write about your favorite movie.

3. Why do you want to attend this school?

Your real reason may be better left unstated ("Because I want to party and screw around for four years"), but the closer to the truth your answer is the more likely you'll be to write something that an admissions officer will enjoy reading. Avoid Joe Bloggs generalities ("to get a good liberal arts education," "to broaden my knowledge"), and think in terms of specifics.

Wake Forest's version of this question is "Why do you think Wake Forest is the best college for you?" Make sure you write about you, not about Wake Forest. They already know about Wake Forest. They want to learn more about you and why you think you're a good fit. Try to find things about Wake Forest that appeal to you. There must be some things or else you wouldn't be applying to go there. Then start thinking about why it appeals to you, and you'll start to get the details about yourself that they're looking for. Again, be specific and make it about you. Don't write, "Because I believe I have something to contribute to your prestigious . . ."

4. How do you see yourself ten years from now?

Joe Bloggs sees himself as a lawyer or a doctor. If you do, too, don't say so. In fact, avoid using this question as an opportunity to describe any type of job you think you'd like to have. This is a tough question, because the temptation to be boring can be overpowering. If you avoid employment as a topic, though, you'll be well ahead of the game. Instead, narrow your focus. Picture yourself doing something a bit unusual, and don't strain to make a direct connection between it and a college education. Just as it is a mistake to act as though your entire life has been building towards your freshman year at College X, you don't want to pretend that you think your college degree will be the sole foundation on which you build the rest of your life.

5. Write about a meaningful activity.

Columbia University's version of this question is, " . . . briefly describe which (school-related or outside) activity/interest represents your most meaningful commitment and why." The best place to start looking for an answer is the truth: Which of your activities really *was* the most meaningful to you? Which was the most fun? Which did you look forward to? Don't say that your most meaningful activity was your service on the Student Council because it taught you the importance of effective leadership. "Effective leadership" was *not* why you liked the student council, assuming that you did. On this type of question, Joe Bloggs tries too hard to make himself seem serious, motivated, and directed. He really ought to be trying to make himself seem interesting.

RECOMMENDATIONS

Most selective colleges ask their applicants to submit two recommendations from teachers. These can have an important bearing on your chances—particularly if they are negative. The following are some guidelines that should help you secure better recommendations:

1. Be prompt:

Teachers have too much to do as it is. Writing recommendations takes a lot of time, especially if you attend a big school and the teachers you ask are popular. Give your recommenders plenty of time. (The earlier you are, the less likely your recommenders are to be buried in recommendation forms already.)

2. Make it easy for them.

When you ask teachers to write recommendations for you, give them everything they need, including your application deadline and a stamped, addressed envelope. Some guidance counselors and books recommend that you also give your recommenders a list of your activities, to remind them of what you've been up to for the last few years. We don't think this is a good idea. Too many recommenders simply rehash students' accomplishments—information that is already in their applications. If your recommender has your brag list sitting there in front of him, he will be unlikely to do much more than turn it into sentences and paragraphs. Admissions officers will wonder why you picked a recommender who obviously knew so little about you.

3. Waive your rights.

You have the legal right to read the stuff colleges have in their files about you. Virtually all recommendation forms include a little box where you can waive this right by signing your name. By all means, waive the right. Colleges won't pay attention to your recommendations if they think the people who wrote them were worried that you would be reading them. Sign the waiver before you give the forms to your teachers.

4. Pick wisely.

The actual content of a recommendation isn't the only important thing about it. To a large degree, a recommendation is also a test of your judgment. If your recommendations are negative or wishy-washy, admissions officers will conclude that you aren't bright enough to pick good recommenders. In general, when choosing recommenders, you should do the following:

- Pick teachers who know and like you.

- Pick teachers who will absolutely positively write positive things about you. This is important enough to discuss openly with your teachers. If you feel uneasy about asking a teacher directly whether he or she will write you a strong recommendation, you can do the same thing indirectly by giving the teacher an out. You might say something like, "I don't want to put you in a spot if you'd prefer not to do this." If the teacher feels uneasy about recommending you, this gives him or her a way to decline without coming right out and telling you you're a jerk. Another way to do the same thing even more indirectly would be to say something like, "I need a strong recommendation, but I know you're busy. Would you have time to write one for me?"

- Pick teachers in fields where your principal interests lie. If you say in your application that you are going to be an English major, at least one or your recommendations should be from an English teacher.

- Pick teachers who are reliable. This is also a test of your judgment. If a teacher doesn't get your recommendation in on time, *you* will be the one who looks bad.

- Pick teachers who are good writers. Nothing is less impressive than a poorly written recommendation.

- If possible and appropriate, pick a teacher who went to the college you want to attend. This probably won't be possible, but you may be able to choose a teacher who went to a similar school, or one of the same caliber. If you're applying to an Ivy League school, a teacher with an Ivy League degree will be in a good position to certify that you are capable of doing Ivy League work. No matter where they went to school, teachers who are familiar with the schools to which you are applying are in a better position to write good recommendations.

5. Send a thank-you note.

Thanking a recommender is good manners. It's also a polite way to remind a forgetful teacher to get on the stick. Send your thank-you note a week or two before the deadline. If writing a note makes you feel uncomfortable, you can thank the recommender in person. It will still serve as a reminder. A hint: Thank your recommender when he is sitting at his desk, not when he is running down the hall. Your reminder will be more likely to produce the desired result if pen and paper are at hand.

6. Don't submit (many) extra recommendations.

Fattening your folder with recommendations from every teacher in your school will just make you look pushy (likewise with recommendations from powerful or famous friends of your parents). We know a student whose father got a U.S. senator to write a recommendation for him. The senator wrote a very flattering letter—about the father. The student was rejected. When the student's guidance counselor asked the college why the student had been rejected, the college said it had been tempted to admit the father, who sounded very interesting, but had decided against it in the end. Letters from famous people almost always seem pushy and show-offy, even if they are informative and sincere.

You *can* submit one or two extra recommendations if they are from people who really do know you well and who really are in a position to say interesting things about you. If you made a big splash at a volunteer job, a letter from your boss could help you. This kind of letter can fill out an admissions officer's image of your personality, revealing the human characteristics that a teacher's recommendations may not.

One of our students was helped considerably by an unsolicited letter from a summer employer. The employer said in his letter that he had given the student a job because he had owed a favor to his father and that he hadn't expected much of him. But the student had worked hard and done magnificently and won the respect of everyone in the office. He said that he would be happy to have the boy in his company full-time and that he could tell he would be a success at whatever he put his hand to. The letter wasn't terribly long, but it was obviously heartfelt and it made a big impression.

INTERVIEWS

Few schools require on-campus interviews. Some don't offer them. Some have elaborate networks of alumni who interview applicants in their areas. Some schools conduct informal interviews with students who need information.

Before you write to an admissions office to arrange "an interview," make sure you understand what kind, if any, the school offers or requires. One of our students told us that the most embarrassing moment of her life was strolling into an admissions office and discovering from a staff member that interviews aren't given.

Most interviews aren't as important as students generally assume. At some colleges, all interviews are handled by the most junior members of the admissions staff. Still, interviews do make impressions. There are certainly examples of students who have been admitted because of a great interview, or rejected because of a horrible one. In most cases, though, the interview tells you more about the school than it tells the school about you. Still, it can't hurt to have as many components of the college application process go as smoothly as possible. Here are a few guidelines for the interview component:

1. Do your homework.

Don't ask questions that are answered in the brochures you've been sent. This means you have to read those brochures. Ugh! Read them one at a time, at breakfast before each interview.

If there is a popular conception of the school (Princeton is isolated, Dartmouth has too many fraternities, Harvard has too little student-teacher contact), *don't* ask about it. Your interviewer will have heard the same question ten billion times. He or she will also have spent the last few weeks reviewing a seemingly endless procession of Joe Bloggses. You don't want to seem off the wall by asking bizarre questions; but even more you don't want to sound exactly like the boring JB who was in there before you.

Don't ask questions if you have no interest in the answers. Unless you have a real reason for wanting to know how many of a college's graduates go on to graduate school, don't ask. The question will make you sound dopey, not smart and serious. And don't read questions from a list. Students who do this look either scatterbrained or nerdy. If you've spent time on campus, ask questions on the information you've gained.

2. Don't give stupid answers.

Before you go to an interview, you need to have a pretty good idea of how you'll answer several stock questions if they're asked. Some of these questions are: Why do you want to go here? What first brought us to your attention? What do you want to major in? What do you want to do with your life?

Most students have a hard time answering questions like this. The trouble with them is that they force you to think specifically about reasons that you probably haven't examined very carefully. But thinking about them is helpful as well as necessary. If you can put your finger on an intelligent and convincing reason why you want to attend a school, not only your interview but also your application will begin to fall into place. The important thing is to be prepared for the "easy ones" so that you don't have to stammer and clear your throat when the admissions officer asks them.

3. Make it easy for your interviewer.

Conviviality, poise, and aplomb are three qualities that have little to do with how good a student you are but a lot to do with how your interview goes. You want to seem bright, interested, mature, and at ease. The more comfortable your interviewer feels at your interview, the better the impression you'll make. If the conversation lags, ask a question.

4. Unless asked specifically—and we mean specifically—don't mention your SAT scores or your grades.

We've said this several times already, but it can't be said enough. One of the most boring and predictable things you can do in an interview is try to sneak in your SAT scores. We even know a student who scored 1400 and said in an interview that he was disappointed in his scores. Obviously he wasn't disappointed. He just wanted to mention those big numbers. The admissions officer thought he was a creep. You will hurt your chances for admission if you make an admissions officer think you are a creep.

A former Ivy League admissions officer once told us about a game she used to play with pushy applicants from certain high schools. She would keep asking questions that she knew would give the students opportunities to work in their SAT scores; then, every time they were about to mention them, she would change the subject. This drove the applicants crazy and kept the admissions officer alert during interviews that she otherwise didn't enjoy. Needless to say, not many of these students received acceptances.

Now, you may say that it's unfair for admissions officers to put so much emphasis on SAT scores and then not want to hear you talk about them. But whoever said life was fair? Don't worry. Your scores are the first thing the admissions officer will look at when he or she picks up your folder. You don't need to wave a flag.

5. Look the part.

Get a respectable haircut. Don't chew gum. Wear nice clothes, but don't look slick (sport coat or skirt, not three-piece suit or party dress). If you're a boy, take out your earring. No matter who you are, clean your fingernails. Brush your teeth. Don't smoke. Wash behind your ears. And in front of your ears. You can go back to being a slob once they let you in.

6. Send your parents to Antarctica.

You definitely shouldn't let your parents try to accompany you to your interview. It's better to keep them out of the building altogether. Parents can only hurt; they never help. We know a brilliant kid who was rejected by a top Ivy League college *solely* because his mother insisted on being present at his interview. Every time the admissions officer would ask a question, the mother would pipe up. The college was worried that the student wouldn't be able to survive his freshman year if they didn't admit his mother as well. (He ended up at another Ivy League college, where he did brilliantly.) What the admissions officer didn't realize was that the student had figured out that the best way to deal with his pushy mom was to let her do what she wanted and not pay any attention. He wasn't dependent on her; she was dependent on him. But that didn't come across. All the admissions officer could see was a mama's boy.

Admissions officers don't like having your mom or dad in the room with you any better than you do. Most will tell parents to wait in the waiting room. But you don't even want this problem to come up. You won't look good if your first contact with an admissions officer involves the admissions officer telling your parents to get lost. If your parents are adamant about wanting to accompany you to your interview itself, don't sign up for an interview.

7. Don't worry about the time.

Students sometimes are told that the sign of a good interview is that it lasts longer than the time allowed for it. Forget about this. During interviewing season, most colleges schedule interviews so tightly that it isn't possible to let one interview run long without screwing up the entire schedule. Don't worry if your interview lasts exactly as long as the secretary said it would. And don't try to stretch out the end of your interview by suddenly becoming long-winded or by asking a lot of questions you don't care about.

8. Save the best for last.

If you have interviews at more than one school, you'll get better as you go along. Try to arrange your schedule so that your first interviews are at the schools you care about least or at any rate the schools you are most likely to get into. You can even schedule interviews at schools in which you have no interest at all, just for the practice. Admissions officers frown on this practice for obvious reasons, but they won't find out.

9. Send a thank-you note afterwards.

Always a good idea. Your note can be quite short, but it shouldn't sound mechanical. As with any good thank-you note, mention a specific. And don't suck up. You might ask your mom to read your note before you send it. And remember, no smiley faces.

QUESTIONS AND ANSWERS

SHOULD I INCLUDE A COPY OF AN A+ PAPER FROM MY ENGLISH CLASS?

No. Many students do this. It almost always backfires. First, admissions officers won't be nearly as interested in your thoughts on *Beowulf* as your English teacher was. Second, if your A+ paper seems boring and poorly written, an admissions officer will begin to have doubts about all those A's in your transcript. Third, no college admissions officer will be happy to be given *more* to read.

That said, of course you should send a copy of a graded paper if the application tells you to submit it.

CAN I USE THE SAME ESSAY ON MORE THAN ONE APPLICATION?

Maybe, although you need to be absolutely certain that the essay fits. Few applications ask exactly the same questions in exactly the same way. Admissions officers are generally familiar with one another's application forms. If your essay only partially fits the question being asked, good admissions officers can often tell which other question (and whose other question) you were answering instead of theirs. Don't give them an opportunity to play this game.

You can probably use at least bits and pieces of the same essay in most or all of your applications. Adapt the material to fit particular questions and particular schools—also particular space requirements. There's no need to start from scratch with every application. After you've borrowed and reworked, read through the entire essay and make sure that, start to finish, your completed essay is appropriate for the particular question.

When essay questions are open-ended enough, students sometimes find that they can slip in a composition written for a class. This is usually not a good idea. Class work has a tendency to sound like class work.

I DON'T CARE WHAT YOU SAY. I'M GOING TO WRITE AN ESSAY THAT'S LONGER THAN THE SPACE ALLOWED FOR IT. WHAT DO YOU THINK OF THAT, HUH?

If you feel you have to do this, and if you are completing your application on paper instead of online, write the entire essay on a separate piece of paper and type "See Attached Essay" in the space provided in the application form. This will keep readers from being confused or having to flip back and forth through your folder. At the top of your attached paper, retype the entire essay question from the application. Make sure everything is clear and clearly labeled.

YOU GAVE A LIST OF BAD ESSAY TOPICS. WHY DON'T YOU GIVE A LIST OF GOOD ESSAY TOPICS?

A good essay topic ceases to be a good essay topic the minute a lot of kids choose it. It becomes a Joe Bloggs essay topic. We do give you a number of suggestions that ought to help you think of interesting topics or approaches, but listing a particular topic in a book effectively kills it. The very best essays are the ones that truly do come from the heart; they don't come from a list. If you follow our guidelines, you should greatly increase your chances of finding a topic or an approach that will show you to your advantage.

IF I WRITE A STUPID ESSAY, WILL I RUIN MY CHANCES?

No. We know of a student who, when asked to write about "a person who has made a difference in your life," filled the entire page with the words "A man called Jesus Christ" in five different colors of crayon. He still got in—and this was a very selective college. That doesn't mean everybody can get away with writing non-essays on forbidden themes in crayon, but it does demonstrate that admissions officers are more understanding of temporary lapses of judgment than they are sometimes believed to be. You shouldn't count on their generosity, though. It's better (and more likely) to be admitted because of your essay than in spite of it.

CHAPTER SIX: MINORITIES, ATHLETES, ARTISTS, AND OTHER SPECIAL CASES

College admissions decisions are made without regard to race, creed, color, or any other factor that has nothing to do with your qualifications as a student—right?

Wrong.

The color of your skin, the size of your family fortune, your religion, your time in the 100-yard dash, and any number of other seemingly extraneous qualities can have a big effect on your chances of being admitted to the school of your choice. Sometimes these factors can help you; sometimes they can harm you. Almost everyone can benefit to some extent by learning what college admissions officers really think.

ETHNIC BACKGROUND

Many colleges are explicit in their quests to increase the number of minority students on campus. Other colleges sometimes claim that their admissions departments are "color-blind" or that they pay no attention to race in deciding who gets in and who is rejected. But this is never true. Ethnic background can make a big difference at virtually every college in the country. Here are some general observations arranged according to particular groups:

1. African Americans

Most selective colleges have tiny percentages of black students. There are many reasons for this, including cultural distortions in the SAT and ACT, poor high school preparation, ignorant admissions officers, and the systematic unfairness of American society. You won't be able to change most of these factors between now and the time you apply to college. But you may be able to change some of them and, in doing so, improve your chances.

Most selective colleges would like to have more African American students than they do, if for no other reason than that they very much want to appear to be unprejudiced. Why don't they simply admit more? There are several reasons. The main one is that they worry that black students, who for various reasons generally attend worse high schools than white students do, won't be adequately prepared. One of the main sources of this concern is the SAT, on which blacks as a group score substantially lower than whites. (Blacks as a group score about 100 points lower on each half of the test than whites do.)

Why do blacks do worse than whites on the SAT? No one really knows, but there are clearly a number of reasons. One is a sort of built-in bias in the test. The SAT is a product of white, upper-middle-class culture, and upper-middle-class whites have a distinct advantage on it. In fact, the correlation between the SAT scores and family income is as strong as the correlation between SAT scores and academic performance at many colleges. Another reason is that predominantly black high schools tend to have less money, fewer resources, worse teachers, and more problems than predominantly white high schools, leaving black students generally less prepared.

Fortunately, as we said in Chapter Two, the SAT is the one significant part of your record that you can do something about in a short time. Careful preparation for the SAT is important for most students, but it is absolutely essential for African

American students. Recruiting of black students by selective colleges is based almost entirely on SAT and PSAT scores. Simply scoring above 650 or so on each half of the test would be enough to virtually guarantee you admission at any college in the country.

Here are some other important guidelines.

- Make sure the admissions committee knows you're Black. (Attach a photograph.) Selective colleges generally have less stringent requirements for Black applicants. In June 2003, the Supreme Court upheld the University of Michigan's policy to consider race to encourage a diverse educational environment that benefits everyone. The court struck down a specific admissions practice which gave all under-represented minorities a pre-set number of points for belonging to those minority groups, but it upheld the concept that, on a case-by-case basis, an admissions committee can weigh an applicant's race in the admissions decision for the purpose of increasing or maintaining diversity. Since African Americans are under-represented at the vast majority of colleges in the country, and since most admission committees are anxious to change that fact, you absolutely want to make sure that the admissions committee knows you're Black.

- Don't be afraid to aim high with some of your applications. You may be able to get into schools that wouldn't accept you if you were white. This is where a college's published statistics might be misleading. If you're Black, you might try to find out the average test scores for accepted Black applicants at that college. If you only look at the overall average, you might be discouraged from applying when, in fact, you might be above the average for your group.

- Investigate the colleges that interest you. Predominantly white colleges can be uncomfortable and sometimes even hostile places for Black students, particularly if they are located in predominantly white areas. We certainly don't want to unnecessarily discourage you from attending a university that is overwhelmingly white, but you might find it helpful to find out not only how many African American students are admitted but also how many stay on to graduate. If the school has a high attrition rate for Blacks (as many do) then you should try to find out what's driving them away.

- Speak with Black students. Find out what their experience has been. The Black population at most selective schools is so small that even talking to a handful of students can give you a fairly complete picture.

2. Hispanic Americans

Being Hispanic can help you, because admitting you will help a college boost its percentage of minority students. You probably won't be able to pass yourself off as a minority, though, if you come from a well-to-do family in Mexico. In general, the guidelines for African Americans apply to you: The easiest way to improve your chances is to get your SAT scores up. At schools where Hispanic students are under-represented minorities, you want to compare your SAT scores not just to those of the overall college population, but to the those of the Hispanic population at that college.

If you have a Hispanic surname (because your father is from Chile, say) but you don't come from a disadvantaged background, don't answer the ethnic-background question on your application.

3. Asian Americans

Asian Americans comprise an increasing proportion of college students nationwide. Many Asian Americans have been extraordinarily successful academically, to the point where some colleges now worry that there are "too many" Asian Americans on their campuses. Being an Asian American can now actually be a distinct disadvantage in the admissions processes at some of the most selective schools in the country.

Increasingly, the standard for affirmative action isn't minority status, but under-represented minority status. Since Asian American populations at many colleges exceed the proportion of Asian Americans to the population of the state or country as a whole, Asian Americans are a minority, but not an under-represented minority, at those colleges.

Many years ago, an education supplement in *The New York Times* contained an article about the academic success of Asian students in America. Along with the article was a sidebar that underscored the disadvantage faced by Asian Americans. "One consequence of Asian Americans' success, many feel, is that they are forced to compete against one another in disciplines in which they excel," the article said. "At Berkeley, Wang Ling-Chi, an associate professor of Asian American Studies, said he knew of several Asian Americans who had been rejected for admission even though their grades were high enough. Each, he said, had wanted to major in electrical engineering, a field already crowded with Asian Americans."

If you are an Asian American—or even if you simply have an Asian or Asian-sounding surname—you need to be careful about what you do and don't say in your application. You need to avoid being an Asian Joe Bloggs.

Asian Joe Bloggs is an Asian American applicant with a very high math SAT score, a low or mediocre verbal SAT score, very high math- or science-related SAT II scores, high math and science grades, few credits in the humanities, few extracurricular activities, an intended major in math or the sciences, and an ambition to be a doctor, an engineer, or a research scientist. The more you sound like this person, the more likely admissions officers will be to treat you as part of the "Asian invasion" and reject your application, or at the very least make you compete against other Asian applicants with similar characteristics, rather than against the applicant pool as a whole.

If you share traits with Asian Joe Bloggs, you should probably pay careful attention to the following guidelines:

- If you're given an option, don't attach a photograph to your application and don't answer the optional question about your ethnic background. This is especially important if you don't have an Asian-sounding surname. (By the same token, if you do have an Asian-sounding surname but aren't Asian, do attach a photograph.)

- Work on your verbal SAT score, take some literature and history courses, and get involved in activities other than math club, chess club, and computer club.

- Do *not* write your application essay about the importance of your family or the positive/negative aspects of living in two cultures. These are Asian Joe Bloggs topics, and they are incredibly popular. Instead, write about something entirely unrelated to your ethnic background.

- Don't say you want to be a doctor, and don't say you want to major in math or the sciences. You don't have to lie. If you have lousy SAT verbal scores, saying you want to be an English major isn't going to help you, either. Just say you're undecided. The point is to distance yourself as much as possible from the stereotype.

These guidelines are less important if you are chiefly interested in less selective schools or if you are applying to schools where *all* the students take only math and science courses and dream of medical or research careers. In fact, Asian Joe Bloggs's high math and science scores can be an advantage in applying to schools below the Ivy League level. Even there, though, the less you sound like the stereotype, the better your chances will be.

RELIGION

Columbia University originally adopted admissions testing (early in this century) in an effort to limit the number of Jews in its student body. The directors of the university believed that if admission were based on the results of an intelligence test, fewer Jews would be admitted, because Jews (according to the directors) were clearly less intelligent than non-Jews. As it turned out, the Jews did better on the intelligence test than the non-Jews.

Although this sort of prejudice is less prevalent and less overt than it was in those days, your religious views and religious background can still affect your admissions chances. Generally speaking, unless you are applying to a school with a clear and stated religious orientation, the less you say about your religious views the better. Students with strong religious beliefs—especially strong religious beliefs that they write about in their application essays—tend to make admissions officers nervous. Write about something else.

ARTISTS, MUSICIANS, AND POETS

Colleges often give special treatment to students with special talents. The simple fact that the university orchestra is short an oboe might be enough to get you into Harvard. (Voice and piano are Joe Bloggs instruments, incidentally. If you want to stand out, take harp lessons.)

Many schools allow you to submit paintings, recordings, and so on for special consideration as part of your application. Other schools, such as Stanford, don't. Be sure you know before you send off your portfolio.

Here are some general guidelines.

- Think small. Send slides, not canvases. Send a *small* selection of your best work, not everything you've ever done. (Comic-book-style drawing doesn't count as art.)

- If your brilliant career as an artist/musician/poet/dancer has brought you into contact with faculty members, consider asking them to recommend you to the admissions committee. One of our students got a powerful recommendation from a poetry professor at a college she wanted to attend. The student had come into contact with the professor in a writing workshop she had attended outside of school. The professor wrote a letter to the admissions committee in support of her, and she was admitted. (She probably would have been admitted anyway, but the letter certainly didn't hurt.) Always follow up with a thank-you note.

- The more professional your slides look, the more impressed the admissions committee will be. This is a corollary of the everything-must-be-typed rule. Have your slides made at a custom photo lab, and submit them in the kinds of plastic sleeves professionals use.

- Published creative writing samples are given more respect than unpublished ones, and outside publications are vastly better than school publications. Published or not, writing samples should be chosen carefully.

It's probably best to avoid forbidden themes (sex, drugs, etc.). You may well have written the freshest work since *Lady Chatterly's Lover*, but that's not going to help you much if your admissions officer only watches G-rated movies. Yet, if you're applying specifically for admission to a creative writing program or to a college with a very liberal reputation, this guideline may not apply to you. Use your best judgment.

- If you submit a tape of your musical performance, be sure it meets the specifications stated in the catalog. While it need not be professionally produced, be sure its quality is as good as possible.

- Don't send volumes of reviews, especially if you are a drama student.

- If you are a dancer, see if a videotape would be reviewed by the dance committee. Submit one only if they really welcome it. In your tape, wear traditional dance attire and don't do anything too weird.

ATHLETES

Everyone knows that great athletic ability can win you a big scholarship at a great athletic school. But it can also get you into the Ivy League.

Almost every college in the country gives preferential treatment to accomplished athletes. How accomplished you have to be in order to get preferential treatment depends on your sport and the school. Your skills as a quarterback might not be enough to win you a scholarship to the University of Alabama, but they might be enough to make Yale overlook your SAT scores, especially if you have scores that are decent enough to work with. Virtually all schools lower their academic requirements for promising athletes. If you don't have what it takes academically to scrape through Ivy League admissions but do have what it takes athletically to start on an Ivy League football team, you could end up at a better school than you may think.

You have to be coveted by a coach before you can get this sort of treatment. If you are a serious prospect and the athletic department doesn't know about you already, visit the school and make an appointment with the coach. If a visit is impossible, write a letter. Ask your high school coach or athletic director to help pave the way or at least help you find the names of the people to whom you should write. A strong recommendation from your high school coach is a must.

Pushing too hard on the athletic angle can be dangerous if you aren't college varsity caliber. If you don't look like a serious prospect, an emphasis on sports in your application could make you look like a "dumb jock," even if your grades and scores are pretty good. Being captain of a team will help you anywhere, though, for the reasons we discussed in Chapter Three.

QUESTIONS AND ANSWERS

IS GENDER A FACTOR IN COLLEGE ADMISSIONS?

Yes. There aren't many single-sex colleges in the country anymore. Most other colleges aim for equal representation of men and women. This doesn't mean that colleges don't pay attention to the gender of their applicants. Men and women are judged by different criteria, and you can take advantage of this in your applications.

Once again, the Joe Bloggs principle is at the heart of it. A boy whose verbal SAT score is higher than his math SAT score stands out, because he contradicts the stereotype that boys' strengths are mathematical and girls' strengths are verbal. Similarly, the girl who was president of her high school math club looks interesting and unusual, while the boy who was president of his math club may look like a nerd. The same principle applies to entire colleges. MIT and Princeton are two schools with strong reputations as male schools. Neither school enrolls as many women as it would like. Because these schools want more women students, women have an advantage in applying. The opposite is true at Vassar. Vassar's image as a school for women persisted after it went coeducational. Men don't apply or enroll at the same rate women do. Thus men have an advantage in admissions—particularly athletes, since male jocks on campus help diminish the school's image as a place for women only.

ARE STUDENTS WITH LEARNING DISABILITIES (LD) TREATED DIFFERENTLY?

Because LD students get to take the SAT untimed, some students work out the following scam: *If I pretend to be LD, I'll get all this extra time on my SAT!* They figure if they can score 1000 timed, a 1300 without time pressure should be a piece of cake. Wrong.

In the first place, to take an untimed SAT, you have to be diagnosed LD. You can't just decide to take it on a whim. In the second place, taking the SAT untimed does not give everyone a significant advantage. At The Princeton Review, we give any student who is considering an untimed SAT two tests—one timed, the other untimed. By comparing the timed score with the untimed score, we get some idea of whether the student should take the SAT untimed.

If you truly are learning disabled, you have two challenges: finding an appropriate school and getting into it. Most colleges aren't set up to deal with serious disabilities, but an increasing number are. If you have always been given special help, you're going to suffer at a school where no such help is given. Many colleges know this, and avoid LD kids.

Being learning disabled, however, does not prevent you from going to college. Indeed, many colleges welcome LD students. By federal law, a college must accept an LD student if he or she is otherwise qualified.

Not every counselor is intimately acquainted with all the colleges offering LD placement. This is a specialized area, so if your school counselor cannot answer all your questions, seek an outside professional. If you want to get information on your own, a good starting place would be *The K&W Guide to Colleges for Students with Learning Disabilities.* This resource not only explains how to go about ensuring that you receive the services and accommodations you need in college, it also profiles over 300 colleges that have significant LD services.

Keep in mind that all too often college faculty resist working with LD students because they do not understand the learning disabled and their needs. If you have a learning disability, you need a college that is committed to educating people like you. A college whose LD program consists solely of tutoring is *not* doing enough. Take a good look at the schools in the *K&W Guide* so that you can make sure you find a school that meets all your needs.

Because you are looking for a good college that will cater to your needs, you should start planning for college earlier than other students. More research is necessary, and campus visits are a must. You may want to begin visiting colleges during your junior year, rather than waiting until your senior year.

CHAPTER SEVEN: FINANCIAL AID

In the final analysis, it all boils down to money. Getting into the greatest college in the world won't do you much good if you can't work out a way to pay for it. There are lots of financial aid opportunities out there, but putting together a financial package, particularly for one of the most expensive private colleges, takes planning.

Joe Bloggs has financial difficulties not because financing isn't available but because he doesn't understand the rules of financial aid. You *can* afford a college education, but if money is tight at home you need to learn how the financial aid process works. The sooner you begin researching this subject, the better. Senior year is no time to start thinking about how to pay for a college education.

THINKING ABOUT MONEY

The price-tag on an elite four-year private college education is now well over $120,000 and even $150,000 at some schools. No one should spend that kind of money without thinking through the consequences. You may believe that going to Yale is worth any sort of sacrifice, including having to scrub out other students' toilets every morning before class, but maybe you'd be happier *not* scrubbing toilets at the University of Connecticut. No book can answer that sort of question for you. But the time to answer it is now, before you enroll and before you start scrubbing.

DO YOUR HOMEWORK

Unless your family is rolling in money, paying for a private college education takes a lot of hard work: sacrifices from your parents, sacrifices from you, and thorough preparation by all of you before you begin. There's a lot of money out there, but you won't find it unless you understand the ins and outs of the aid process. We strongly suggest that you supplement this book with several resource books devoted exclusively to securing financial aid. Of course, it's also well worth your time to go to www.princetonreview.com. The more money you need, the more important it is for you to begin researching financial aid as early as possible.

You won't be surprised to learn that we think the best guide to financial aid is a book we put out called *Paying for College Without Going Broke*. It will teach you how to maximize your financial aid eligibility, how to develop some short-term and long-term college funding strategies, and how to complete the all-important Free Application for Federal Student Aid (FAFSA).

THERE ARE LOWER-COST ALTERNATIVES

One of the easiest ways to afford a college education is to get a cheaper college education. If you don't believe a good education can be had for less than $15,000 a year, think again. A number of first-rate colleges and universities in this country that don't have quite the cachet of the Ivy League schools but offer comparable educations at substantially less cost. If you happen to be lucky enough to live in a state with an excellent university system, you could be in luck. For example, did you know that Cornell University—an Ivy League school—consists of four private colleges and three public colleges in the State University of New York system? By attending one of the SUNY divisions of Cornell, a student gets access to the same superb facilities, the same top-notch professors, and receives an Ivy League degree for a fraction of the cost of a private university. Other examples abound. The University of Texas at Austin and The University of North Carolina at Chapel Hill are incredible bargains for in-state students, and not half-bad for out-of-staters at well.

HOWEVER, DON'T JUST ASSUME YOU CAN'T AFFORD AN EXPENSIVE SCHOOL

You should remember that the nation's richest, most elite private universities aren't just for the rich and elite. Students from families with modest incomes often assume that the prestigious private schools are out of their league financially. In fact, it is the wealthy schools that have the most money to spend on financial aid. If you have the necessary academic credentials, you may be pleasantly surprised to find that the most prestigious school on your list is also the one that offers you the most attractive aid package. It doesn't always happen that way, of course, but it is *always* true that private schools with small endowments per student have a much harder time providing aid to those who need it. Richer schools can be more generous than poorer ones.

BARGAINING

Even the most competitive schools will sweeten aid packages for highly desirable candidates. This means that the financial aid package a student first receives from a college is not necessarily as high as the college is prepared to go. Don't think you can't bargain. You can, especially if your credentials make you very marketable.

STAYING UP-TO-DATE

The financial aid picture is changing all the time. Changes in tuition, changes in aid opportunities, and changes in tax laws can make good books obsolete in a hurry. Always check the copyright date of any financial aid reference book you find in the library. A book or edition that's even a year old can be misleading. That's why we update *Paying for College* so frequently, and why we post further updates on our website.

FINANCIAL SAFETY SCHOOLS

As we have said before, no college is completely "needblind" in weighing applications. Your ability to pay can affect your chance of being admitted. A few colleges sift through their tentative acceptances before mailing them and weed out the *marginal* candidates with extremely large aid needs.

The point is not that your family should put itself in financial jeopardy to pay for your education. You should be honest and realistic as you assess what kind of an aid package you will need in order to be able to afford a particular school—and then balance that with a realistic appraisal of how badly that school is going to want you. It is a good idea to apply to at least one school where you will not be considered marginal.

Everyone knows about the concept of a "safety school." Students who need financial aid to help pay for college must pick a *financial* safety school as well. A financial safety school is not just a school that is likely to accept you, but a school that is either cheap enough for your family to afford without financial aid, or a school that wants you so badly they will give you an extremely good package.

Some colleges state right up front in their literature: If you have SAT scores above X and a GPA above Y, then we are prepared to offer you a full scholarship. Other schools offer merit scholarships based on high school academic performance. It may surprise you to learn that you don't always have to be an academic superstar to qualify. In some cases these scholarships are awarded to students with B averages.

DEBT

The federal government's Stafford Student Loan program lends tens of billions every year. This is wonderful, of course, but there is something you should always bear in mind as you apply for college—student loans eventually have to be paid back. As many as half of the students who graduate from college this year will graduate in debt. Recent college graduates often have the feeling that they go to work only to pay taxes and pay off their college debts. Once those two items are taken care of, there often isn't much left for the other things in life—such as food and rent.

In other words, the decision to go into debt should be made carefully.

PRE-MEDS BEWARE!

Keeping your debt burden to a minimum is especially important if you plan to go on to graduate or professional school. Suppose you want to be a dentist. After four years of college you have four or five years of dental school. By the time you're ready to begin practicing, you could easily be a hundred thousand dollars in debt. If you want to go into private practice, you could easily go *another* hundred thousand dollars in the red just setting up your office. Then, of course, you'll need a place to live.

HOW THE FINANCIAL AID PROCESS WORKS

Applying to college with a need for financial aid is a two-step process: You apply for admission and you apply for aid. When a college decides to accept you, the school's financial aid office will put together a financial aid package to make up the difference between what the school actually costs (the "sticker price") and what you can afford to pay (called the Expected Family Contribution, or EFC).

The package will generally consist of some combination of outright grants, loans, and a guaranteed job for you on campus during the school year. Obviously, the more money you can get in the form of an outright grant or a work-study job, the better off you're going to be, because that money won't have to be paid back later on.

THE FAFSA AND OTHER FORMS

How do colleges know how much your family can afford to contribute? In January of your senior year, you'll fill out a FAFSA (Free Application for Federal Student Aid). You and your parents will answer a bunch of questions about your income during the previous year, how many people live in your household, what sorts of assets you have, and so on. You'll have to fill this form out every January if you want to qualify for need-based money. This form is required in addition to financial aid and scholarhip forms that each individual college may require you to fill out. It's a long and messy process, but it's worth it if you get some money.

In addition to the FAFSA, some colleges may require you to fill out the financial aid PROFILE form as well, brought to you by the same people who brought you the SAT—the College Board.

FILE YOUR FORMS EARLY

As always, beware of creeping deadlines. Your various financial aid forms at the colleges may not all be due at the same time, and they may be due at different times from the FAFSA, which is due in March. Even more important, your chances of receiving an attractive aid offer, or any offer at all, may depend on how early you submit your forms. Colleges have a tendency to be more generous with aid early in the process and gradually to become stingy as resources are depleted. If you wait to apply until after the deadline, the college may have nothing left to offer you. This can also affect your chances of admission. Faced with the choice of rejecting you or accepting you with an inadequate aid offer, the college may elect to reject you.

SO HOW ARE THE FAFSA AND OTHER FORMS USED TO DETERMINE MY ELIGIBILITY?

The information on the FAFSA is analyzed by computer, and the results of the analysis, along with the computer's estimate of how much your family can afford to pay toward college, is sent to the schools you have applied to in much the same way that your SAT or ACT scores are reported. You will also receive a summary of your report. Be sure to check it for errors, which are not uncommon.

You'll be told what your expected family contribution is. The schools will take the cost of attending for one year, including room and board, and then subtract the EFC. Whatever is left over is called "your need." The school then puts together a package of aid to help you meet that need. You'll have the option of accepting or rejecting each line item of that offer. If the school's aid package doesn't cover the entire need, you'll have an amount that is labeled "unmet need."

SOURCES OF AID

Many sources of financial aid allow colleges to meet as much of your need as possible. Some you know about already, some you probably don't. As we mentioned earlier, a financial aid package usually breaks down into three parts: outright grants from the college itself or the government, loans, and guaranteed jobs on campus. The constant in every package is your family's contribution. If you are eligible for aid and you suddenly win a thousand-dollar scholarship from the local Lions' Club, the thousand dollars probably won't go to your parents, enabling them to reduce their contribution; it will go straight to the college's financial aid office which will then reduce the amount of grant money they were going to give you. An outside scholarship may enhance your desirability with the colleges, but it may not reduce your family contribution. Different colleges use different rules regarding how to apply scholarships to need-based financial aid packages. Obviously, this is something you'll want to check into at the colleges you're interested in attending.

ALL OFFERS ARE NOT EQUAL

The composition of an aid package is at least as important as the total amount. Suppose your family can afford to contribute $4,000 a year to your college education, and you've been accepted by two schools whose costs are approximately $8,000 a year. Both schools come up with aid packages worth $4,000 a year. But the packages are not the same.

Here's how they break down.

Package A

Outright grant: $2,000

Campus job: $1,000

Loan: $1,000

Package B

Outright grant: $3,000

Campus job: $1,000

College A expects you to borrow $1,000. This loan is part of the financial aid equation for that school. College B, however, wants you badly enough to offer you $3,000 outright. In combination with a job worth $1,000, this takes care of your financial needs—and you'll graduate without debt.

Weighing financial aid offers can get a lot more complicated than that. You and your parents will have to work together closely and think realistically about the consequences of your decisions. The more attractive you are to a school in comparison with other applicants, the sweeter their aid offer is likely to be. Deciding which offer to accept is sometimes a matter of deciding between a better school and a better aid package. If two comparably rated colleges have accepted you, but one school gave you substantially more money in aid, it may be possible to negotiate a better package with the other school.

SOURCES OF AID II

The following is a survey of the most important sources of financial aid. We'll cover the more unusual sources first, and then get down to the nitty-gritty of things like government entitlement programs and sources of loans.

UNUSUAL SOURCES

SCHOLARSHIPS THROUGH TESTING, PART ONE

If you take Advanced Placement courses and do well on the tests, you could earn—regardless of your financial need—the equivalent of an outright grant worth twenty-five percent of your four-year college costs, including tuition, room and board, books, beer, expenses, and everything else.

How?

Simply by doing well enough on your AP tests to earn academic credits at the college where you enroll. Students with top AP scores are sometimes awarded as much as a full year's worth of college credit. This enables them to graduate in three years and save a full year's worth of college costs.

Not all colleges do this, but many do. And some grant credit for AP scores that are really quite low. Granting AP credit lets the colleges feel generous: They can give the equivalent of big scholarships at no cost to themselves. And for students, the potential return on an investment in AP test fees is enormous. The only negative consideration is that starting college as a sophomore can be disorienting (also less fun—three years of fooling around instead of four). But the AP program remains a source of financial aid that many students overlook.

AP tests, naturally, are a College Board/ETS program. A similar program, run by the same company, is the College Level Examination Program (CLEP). CLEP tests are somewhat easier than the AP tests, and are not accepted by all colleges.

SCHOLARSHIPS THROUGH TESTING, PART TWO

The PSAT, which is usually given early in junior year, not only gives you practice for the SAT but also enters you in an aid lottery called the National Merit Scholarship Program. Students who score extremely well on the test may qualify for scholarships of various kinds, some of which are based on need and some of which are not. Even if you don't win money, being designated a finalist, semifinalist, or letter of commendation winner can improve your admission chances substantially. Get the details from your guidance counselor (and practice for the PSAT).

Some colleges now offer outright awards to students who score high on the PSAT or SAT, regardless of their financial need. Others offer scholarships based on high class ranks. These awards are essentially a marketing tool: The schools that offer them are typically competitive, sub-Ivy League schools that want to make themselves look more selective by enrolling some students with big test scores. If you have a knack for taking ETS tests, it can be worth a good deal of money. Talk to your guidance counselor, check information on websites, and read the information colleges send you.

THE MILITARY

"We're not a company; we're your country." Ever since the creation of the GI Bill, which enabled returning soldiers to attend college at the end of World War II, military service has provided a way for young people to pay for college educations. Of course, there's a very big string attached: You have to pay for your financial aid by serving in the military. A military commitment is no joke. It lasts a long time, once you've signed up for it you can't weasel your way out of it, and, depending on the state of the world, you could get shot at. But there are rewards as well. For example, winning a Reserve Officer Training Corps (ROTC) scholarship can be worth as much as four years' tuition at a private college—in addition to a monthly living allowance. To avoid missing out on any military options, you should check out these programs as early as junior year in high school.

THE COLLEGES THEMSELVES

As colleges have become more and more competitive in their search for good students, they have also become more innovative and aggressive in devising ways to help students pay their tuitions. Some of the current offerings: flexible payment plans, inexpensive loans, extended payment plans, and prepayment plans.

Sorting through these innovative plans requires a good bit of homework. Many are just gimmicks designed to attract attention. But some are genuinely helpful to parents in need. It's worth remembering that colleges want good students just as much as students want degrees. Do the research and ask questions if you are confused.

SOURCES OF LOANS

There are billions of dollars available each year in loans either subsidized or guaranteed by the federal government. More loans are available from state governments, still more are available from banks and other financial institutions, and even more are available from colleges. Now, if only you didn't have to pay them back . . .

1. Stafford Loans

These are relatively low-interest loans guaranteed and subsidized by the federal government. For new borrowers, rates are variable, currently with an 8.25 percent cap. You pay no interest while you're in school or for six months after you graduate (taxpayers pick up the tab), and you can take up to ten years to pay the money back. Stafford loans are also available for graduate students.

Unfortunately, you can't just decide, "I'm going to take out a Stafford Loan." These loans are awarded only as part of the aid packages put together by colleges. And like the rest of an aid package, Stafford Loans are awarded based on need. Once the college decides to let you take out one of these loans, you have to apply to a bank to actually get the money.

2. Perkins Loans

These are loans made by colleges with money provided by the federal government. The interest rate is quite low—currently five percent. As with the Stafford Loans, interest payments are picked up by the government during school and repayment doesn't begin until after graduation.

The catch is that, again, Perkins Loans are awarded only as part of an aid package, and are based solely on need. College financial aid officers have the only say in deciding which students qualify for these loans.

Aside from outright grant money, the Perkins Loan is the best form of financial aid available. Students should never turn down a Perkins Loan.

3. Parent Loans for Undergraduate Students (PLUS)

These are loans available to all parents of college students, no matter what their income level. The interest rate is higher (currently the cap is at 9 percent). The repayment period is ten years, but there is no interest subsidy and repayment begins immediately. Similar loans are available for independent students (those not supported by parents) and graduate students.

While Stafford and Perkins loans are meant to help make up the difference between what a family can afford to pay for college (called the Family Contribution) and what the college actually costs, PLUS loans are designed to help families having trouble paying the Family Contribution itself. These loans are *not* part of the aid packages awarded by the colleges.

Most commercial banks offer PLUS loans, but parents must be judged credit-worthy in order to qualify.

4. State Loans

All 50 states and the District of Columbia have financial aid programs that award both grants and student loans. In most cases, to qualify for state aid, you must live and go to school in that state. In many states, you automatically apply for state aid when you fill out the FAFSA or the PROFILE standardized aid forms, although a few states have their own forms. In either case, if you qualify for state grants or loans, they will appear in the aid packages put together for you by the colleges that accept you.

State aid should not be taken lightly. Some states provide up to $4,000 per year per student.

Here's a listing of the websites for the state agencies. If we weren't able to find a website for a state, we have listed a phone number instead.

Alabama www.ache.state.al.us

Alaska www.state.ak.us/acpe/

Arizona contact the college's financial aid office

Arkansas www.arkansashighered.com

California www.csac.ca.gov

Colorado www.state.co.us/cche

Connecticut www.ctdhe.org

Delaware www.doe.state.de.us/high-ed

District of Columbia 202-698-2400

Florida www.firn.edu/doe/bsfa

Georgia www.gsfc.org

Hawaii 808-956-8213

Idaho www.idahoboardofed.org

Illinois www.collegezone.com

Indiana www.in.gov/ssaci/

Iowa www.iowacollegeaid.org

Kansas www.kansasregents.com

Kentucky www.kheaa.com

Louisiana www.osfa.state.la.us

Maine www.famemaine.com

Maryland www.mhec.state.md.us

Massachusetts www.osfa.mass.edu

Michigan www.mi-studentaid.org

Minnesota www.mheso.state.mn.us

Mississippi 601-432-6997

Missouri www.mocbhe.gov

Montana www.mgslp.state.mt.us

Nebraska www.ccpe.state.ne.us

Nevada www.nde.state.nv.us

New Hampshire www.state.nh.us/postsecondary

New Jersey www.hesaa.org

New Mexico www.nmche.org

New York www.hesc.com

North Carolina www.cfnc.org

North Dakota www.ndus.edu/student_info

Ohio www.regents.state.oh.us/sgs

Oklahoma www.okhighered.org/student-center

Oregon www.osac.state.or.us

Pennsylvania www.pheaa.org

Rhode Island www.riheaa.org

Tennessee www.state.tn.us/tsac

Texas www.thecb.state.tx.us

Utah www.utahsbr.edu

Vermont www.vsac.org

Virginia www.schev.edu

Washington www.hecb.wa.gov

West Virginia www.hepc.wvnet.edu

Wisconsin www.heab.state.wi.us

Wyoming www.uwyo.edu

5. Commercial Loans

Banks are in the business of lending money, of course. If you have to go the ordinary bank route, though, you generally leave the world of below-market interest rates. Check with the financial aid offices at your prospective colleges to find out about alternative loan programs available for those schools.

SOURCES OF OUTRIGHT GRANTS

1. Pell Grants

Pell grants are cash grants from the federal government paid to undergraduate students who come from low-income families. You automatically apply for the Pell simply by signing your name on your PROFILE or FAFSA form.

The income requirements to be eligible for a Pell Grant are pretty tough. If you don't qualify, don't panic. There are other types of grant money available, which are described below:

2. Supplemental Educational Opportunity Grant

This is another federal grant program. Although the money comes from the government, the colleges themselves determine who gets these grants based on your need relative to the need of the other students at the school.

3. Grants from the Colleges Themselves

This is the big question mark. Virtually all private colleges and many state colleges offer their own awards. If a college really wants a student, the college may give the student a grant in any amount ranging from a few dollars all the way up to a full scholarship. Some schools award their grants solely based on demonstrated need. Other schools award some merit-based grants as well. The richer the school, of course, the more money will be available.

4. Clubs and Organizations

Lions Clubs, alumni groups, garden clubs, and many civic and other organizations provide scholarship money for college students. Such awards are usually small. You shouldn't waste a lot of time scouring the countryside for a few hundred dollars. But be aware of opportunities in your own backyard. If the Loyal Brotherhood of Hyenas has a scholarship, and your father is a Loyal Hyena, you could be in luck.

You should also be aware that many companies—including, perhaps, the ones your mom and dad work for—provide money for college. Your own employer may even have such a program. Check around.

On the other hand, remember that colleges seldom allow outside scholarships to be used to lower the Family Contribution. Instead, the outside scholarship money will simply take the place of grant money the college would probably have given you anyway.

QUESTIONS AND ANSWERS

SHOULD I HIRE A SCHOLARSHIP SEARCH SERVICE?

No. Over 90 percent of scholarship money is administered by the colleges themselves, and you automatically apply for it when you apply to the schools. For the remaining 10 percent, you can go online for free. Of course, we strongly recommend that you go to www.princetonreview.com, where you can search for tons of them.

SHOULD A FAMILY DO SOME PREPARING BEFORE THEY FILL OUT THE STANDARDIZED FORMS?

Over half the people in the United States would not dream of doing their own taxes, and yet most parents sit down to fill out FAFSA (which are more complicated than the 1040 IRS form) with no help aside from a large pot of coffee and a No. 2 pencil.

The decisions the colleges will make on the basis of your answers to the questions on these forms are too important for you to fill out the forms without understanding the *process* of financial aid. Parents who understand the ins and outs of the aid process can increase their aid eligibility by thousands of dollars. Necessarily, this chapter could only hit the highlights of that process. We strongly recommend that you do some additional reading, as we've noted earlier.

SHOULD A FAMILY HIRE A PROFESSIONAL TO HELP FILL OUT THE FINANCIAL AID FORMS?

A good financial aid consultant, or an accountant who is familiar with the arcane rules of financial aid, can increase your aid eligibility as well as help you put together a long-range college fund. Check around. The financial aid center at www.princetonreview.com will guide you through the forms and allow you to calculate your EFC, as well as compare financial aid offers from colleges, so it's an excellent place to start.

SHOULD I EVEN BOTHER APPLYING FOR FINANCIAL AID IF MY PARENTS MAKE A LOT OF MONEY?

It is astonishing how much money you have to earn NOT to qualify for aid. It is *always* worth a try.

DOES APPLYING FOR AID JEOPARDIZE MY CHANCES OF ADMISSION?

While colleges may not be completely need-blind in their souls, the only time need affects admission is when a *marginal* student has a *high* need.

If you are a "high-need" student, you really don't have a choice—you have to apply for aid. Just be sure to apply to at least one school where your academic profile fits into the top third of last year's entering class, and remember to apply to a financial safety school as well.

IS A COLLEGE EDUCATION REALLY WORTH ALL THE TROUBLE IT TAKES TO GET ONE?

Yes.

APPENDIX

THE NINTH GRADE CHECKLIST

The following checklist is from the *College Admissions Handbook Series: 9th Grade: Understanding High School.* You should check out this handbook if you are near the beginning of your freshman year. Use this checklist to make sure you do everything that needs to be done.

☐ I know the grading scale that is used at my high school.

☐ I know the grade point conversion system (that tells me how many grade points each letter is worth) that is used at my high school.

☐ I know the graduation requirements of my high school.

☐ I know how many credits I need to graduate.

☐ I understand that colleges will want me to do more than the minimum graduation requirements and will want me to challenge myself by enrolling and doing well in tough classes.

☐ I know who my counselor is, and he or she knows who I am.

☐ I have tried to develop friendly relationships with my teachers and counselor.

☐ I understand that the colleges that I apply to will see the classes that I took during 9th grade, the grades that I earned in those classes, the GPA that I earned each semester, and my cumulative GPA.

☐ I understand how GPA is calculated.

☐ I understand that my cumulative GPA is probably the biggest factor in college admissions.

☐ I know all of the activities that are offered and organizations that I am interested in pursuing.

☐ I have written down my goals and have set my priorities.

☐ I have set aside some time on my calendar to study every single day.

☐ I keep track of the grades in my classes so that I always know where I stand and if I need to work harder to improve my grade to reach my goals.

☐ I attempt every assignment, project, and test so that I don't earn any zeros.

☐ I try to earn the highest grades that I possibly can.

☐ I have completed my Profile on ECOS, and begun exploring the college, majors, and career tools.

Tenth Grade Checklist

The following checklist is from the *College Admissions Handbook Series: 10th Grade: The College Path.* You should check out this handbook if you are near the beginning of your sophomore year. Use this checklist to make sure you do everything that needs to be done.

By the end of your sophomore year, you should accomplish everything on the list below as follows:

☐ I have tried to earn the highest grades I possibly can.

☐ I have actively chosen challenging courses for my junior year.

☐ I understand the differences among four year colleges, two year colleges, and trade schools.

☐ I understand that admission to four year colleges varies from college to college. Some are guaranteed admission, while others are selective or highly selective.

☐ I understand the credentials that selective and highly selective colleges will expect me to have.

☐ I understand what a college major is.

☐ I have thought about some careers and majors I might be interested in.

☐ I have explored careers, majors, and colleges on ECOS.

☐ I have taken the Career Assessment on ECOS.

☐ I understand the level of education that I will be expected to complete in order to pursue the careers that I am currently interested in.

☐ I have saved the careers, majors, and colleges that interest me most in my ECOS Locker.

☐ I have updated my Profile in my ECOS Portfolio to reflect changes to my cumulative GPA, personal information, and test scores.

☐ I have thought about my extracurricular activities and considered the ones I want to give the highest priority to during my junior and senior years.

☐ I understand the purpose of the PSAT.

☐ I have asked my counselor if and when I will be taking the PSAT.

☐ If the PSAT is offered at my high school to sophomores, I have taken it seriously, because good things might come my way as a result of high scores.

ELEVENTH GRADE CHECKLIST

The following checklist is from the *College Admissions Handbook Series: 11th Grade: The College Admissions Process*. You should check out this handbook if you are near the beginning of your junior year. Use this checklist to make sure you do everything that needs to be done.

By the end of your junior year, you should be able to say that you've accomplished everything on the list below, especially if you intend to apply to a selective or highly selective college:

- ☐ I understand the college admissions process. In other words, I understand all the things I will need to send to colleges to which I intend to apply.

- ☐ I understand the difference between early admission and regular admission and realize that if I choose to apply early, I'm going to need to finish all of the application materials in October of my senior year.

- ☐ I have used the College Directory and Scholarship Search Directory on Ecos to find out information about colleges and scholarships that interest me.

- ☐ I have used the College Search and Scholarship Search on ECOS to find colleges and scholarships that I didn't previously know about but that might be good matches for me.

- ☐ I have found a range of schools that I am interested in. If I'm interested in some schools that cost a lot of money, I've also found some schools that don't cost as much. I have used College Strategy on ECOS to help me evaluate the colleges in my locker.

- ☐ I know the admissions statistics for the schools to which I intend to apply: the average GPA of admitted students, the average test scores, etc.

- ☐ I have taken the ACT or the SAT at least once.

☐ I have determined if I want to take the ACT or SAT again during my senior year.

☐ I have checked to see if any of the colleges I am interested in attending require the SAT IIs, and if so, I have either taken the SAT IIs during my junior year or intend to register for them in October of my senior year.

☐ I have given some thought to who I would like to ask to write my letters of recommendation.

☐ I have thought about some potential topics for college application essays.

☐ I have visited colleges that I'm interested in attending or have made plans to visit colleges. If I couldn't visit them because they are too far away, I have researched them and emailed the Admissions Office if all of my questions that weren't answered on ECOS or on their websites.

☐ I intend to read the *12th Grade Handbook* over the summer so that I can hit the ground running when my senior year starts.

NOTES

NOTES

NOTES

NOTES